LIFE@WORK

A Handbook on Marketplace Success for People of Faith

JOHN C. MAXWELL

STEPHEN R. GRAVES

THOMAS G. ADDINGTON

NELSON IMPACT

A Division of Thomas Nelson Publishers

Since 1798

www.thomasnelson.com

Published in Nashville, Tennessee, by Thomas Nelson, Inc.

Scripture quotations identified NIV are from the *Holy Bible,* New International Version. Copyright © 1973, 1978, 1984 by International Bible Society. Used by permission of Zondervan Bible Publishers. NIV and *New International Version* are registered in the United States Patent and Trademark Office by International Bible Society.

Scripture quotations identified MSG are taken from *The Message,* copyright © 1992, 1994, 1996, 2000, 2001, 2002 by NavPress Publishing Group. Used by permission. All rights reserved.

Scripture quotations identified NASB are taken from the *New American Standard Bible.* Copyright © 1960, 1962, 1963, 1968, 1971, 1972, 1973, 1975, 1977, 1995 by The Lockman Foundation. Used by permission. (www.Lockman.org)

Scripture quotations identified NLT are taken from *The Holy Bible,* New Living Translation. Copyright © 1986 by Tyndale House Publishers, Wheaton, Illinois, 60189. Used by permission. All rights reserved.

Published in association with Yates & Yates, LLP, Attorneys and Counselors, Orange, California.

ISBN: 1-4185-0328-2

Printed in the United States of America
1 2 3 4 5 6 — 08 07 06 05

Acknowledgments

Stephen Caldwell
Sam Hannon

Thanks for all your help in transferring the concepts first outlined in the Life@Work trade book into this interactive handbook format. It is a special experience to work with someone who delivers skill, models serving, displays character and evidences calling in the details of their daily work. Our interchange with you took all the ideas of this book and attached them to a local voice and familiar face. Thanks again.

Thank you to the hundreds of men and women of faith who helped us shape the thinking of this book. Most of the stories used in this book have one of you in mind. While the stories are true, some details in some accounts have been changed to honor your privacy.

Contents

CALLING@WORK

SERVING@WORK

CHARACTER@WORK

CONCLUSION

The Life@Work Test

Assess how sharp both edges of your Life@Work are by answering yes or no to the following statements:

- My skill set is sharper today than it was three years ago and my boss would agree.

  Yes _____ No _____

- My faith has made me "more valuable" to my company, not "less valuable."

  Yes _____ No _____

- I have a reputation at work of being someone who sacrificially helps others succeed without needing any credit for it.

  Yes _____ No _____

- My coworkers see me as a person settled, engaged and fulfilled in my work station.

  Yes _____ No _____

- I am as energized in my work life as I am in my ministry world.

  Yes _____ No _____

- I am the same person on Monday at work as I am Sunday at church.

  Yes _____ No _____

- I have learned to stand firm in my convictions regardless of the setting or circumstance.

  Yes _____ No _____

- My life is enough salt and light to cause my coworkers and neighbors to find Jesus.

    Yes _____ No _____

- Even if I became independently wealthy, I would still keep working.

    Yes _____ No _____

- I am actively helping the leadership in my church to better understand and engage the workplace.

    Yes _____ No _____

If you answered "yes" to:

9–10 Your Life@Work sword is a doubly-sharp penetrating presence.

6–8   Your blade is dull.

3–5   Your blade is broken.

0–2   The enemy has stolen your sword.

CHAPTER I

REFORGING OUR FRAGMENTED LIFE@WORK

"IT IS NOT, TRULY SPEAKING, THE LABOR THAT IS DIVIDED;
BUT THE MEN: DIVIDED INTO MERE SEGMENTS OF MEN—
BROKEN INTO SMALL FRAGMENTS AND CRUMBS OF LIFE."

—JOHN RUSKIN

✸ DRIVING THOUGHT

God's original blueprint for our Life@Work calls us to be comfortable and capable in both the spiritual arena and the commercial arena.

✸ DRILLING DOWN

Charles Antonio Bordini III was high-spirited, uncomfortably transparent, and voraciously hungry to learn. He was new to Chicago and new to the life of faith, but he was developing a reputation as a mover and shaker in Christian circles to match the reputation he already had in the corporate world.

If there was a major financial deal going down, Charlie was in the middle of it. Charlie was a player. Now that he was a Christian, he was becoming a player in the world of faith, as well.

Hanging out with Charlie reminded me of eating at my favorite Italian restaurant. Loud. Chaotic. Rich. Charlie's personality created a self-charging level of energy and enthusiasm. And as Carlos Santana said, "There is nothing more contagious on this planet than enthusiasm."

Not long ago, after speaking to a large gathering of young executives over breakfast in Chicago, I hung around to meet with the board of directors of the organization hosting the event. They wanted me to field a few questions on the faith and work movement. To no one's surprise, Charlie had just been added to the board.

"I have a question," Charlie said, during a lull in the conversation. "I am not sure, but I think I have a dilemma. A few of my employees lately have told me that there are two different Charlie's that come to work. Depending upon which Charlie walks through the door, they can tell exactly what kind of day it's going to be."

His employees, he explained, sometimes see him as "Charlie Love." On other days, however, they see him as "Charlie Money."

"Charlie Love is the Christian Charlie," he said. "He is full of patience and understanding. He cares about the bigger things in life. They like Charlie Love. When he comes to work, they know it's going to be a good day."

And Charlie Money?

"According to them, Charlie Money is all business. He walks in cracking Pharaoh's whip, driving the organization for results, pushing people and demanding performance. He is satisfied with nothing less than excellence. Charlie Money, as you might imagine, is not so popular. When he comes through the door, everybody battens down the hatches."

Sheepishly Charlie admitted, "My folks say I am schizophrenic. To be honest, I think they're probably right and I am not sure what to do about it."

One of Charlie's peers in business spoke up. "Charlie, I know *exactly* what you need to do. Charlie Love needs to drag Charlie Money down to the basement," he said emphatically, "and *kill* him!"

If you can't kill him, the friend added, then "chain him up down there and never let him out." That is *the* only way to survive. He even quoted a couple of Scriptures to prove his point.

The room was dead silent. Charlie sat stunned, a puzzled look plastered on his brow. You could tell his mind was processing what he had just been told.

Then, all eyes turned toward me.

I hesitated, a little unsure if they were ready to hear what I was really thinking. Then, recognizing that this was a gathering that valued truth over tact, I plunged in.

"Charlie, I could not disagree more."

"No offense," I added, "but I simply believe our friend sitting across the table from you is dead wrong. I have another alternative for you: 'Charlie Love' needs to meet 'Charlie Money,' and they need to get into the same skin."

MAKING EVALUATION

Charlie Love and Charlie Money were at an impasse. Charlie Love felt called to be a person of faith, and Charlie Money felt called to make a living. Neither knew how to find the secret to be just "Charlie," a new creation made to instinctively live out God's glory and excellence in every area of life.

Does Charlie look familiar? Even if you have never met Charlie, you probably know him. You've seen him in the mirror.

There are Charlie's in sales, on the shop floors, in home offices—just about anywhere people work. Some Charlie's are men, and others are women. What they all have in common is an identity crisis at work that is at epidemic levels. At one time or another, all of us feel a strain between our soul and our job. And harnessing those two appetites into one person is no easy task.

This schism between Charlie Love and Charlie Money manifests itself in a number of common feelings. Which of the following do you most identify with?

You're fatigued from juggling two worlds. Neither world seems to understand or value the whole of who you are. Work says your faith is strictly personal—leave it at home! Christian culture says working for the world is a waste—give it up! Both are isolated from one another. Yet, they both demand your allegiance. You feel like a child of divorce caught in the middle of two parents. You have two different homes. Different parts of you live in each one. You want a life that is whole again. Sometimes you wish you could just get your two worlds to talk to one another!

You need more meaning from your work. You want your life to count. Often, however, you look back at the end of the week and see little that will last until eternity. You want to work for something bigger than yourself. Katherine Graham once said, "To love what you do and feel that it matters—how could anything be more fun?" You know one thing for sure: Doing something that you feel doesn't matter, definitely *isn't* fun.

You need a clear picture of what being a Christian on the job looks like. You know your faith should shape your work. You just don't understand what that really looks like. What *is* a "Christian work-life"? You know what it means to be a follower of Jesus. You also know your profession. You just want to know what the two have to do with each other.

YOU NEED A FAITH THAT MAKES A DIFFERENCE IN YOUR LIFE AND YOUR JOB. You are committed to making Jesus Lord of all your life. You work in an office culture, however, that at its worst is hostile to God and at its best is indifferent. You face the daunting challenges of navigating a minefield of obstacles, any one of which could sink your career tomorrow. Frankly, your work life needs all the help it can get. If your faith can't help, then what hope do you have?

YOU FEEL LIKE YOU'RE RECEIVING NO HELP CONNECTING YOUR WORLDS. It seems like you're in this by yourself. Your work life is off the church's radar screen, clueless, it seems, about the problems you face Monday through Friday. Every once in while you hear a sermon exhorting you to be more Christ-like at work or encouraging you to be a more active witness, but it seldom goes deeper than that.

❀ TAKING ACTION

1. Do you count yourself as a person of faith and follower of Christ like Charlie? Can you relate to constantly toggling between Charlie Love and Charlie Money, never quite sure when to turn one on and the other off? How so?

_____

_____

_____

_____

_____

2. How do you relate to the following feelings that resulted from Charlie's attempt to integrate his faith@work?

Feeling One: "I am tired of juggling two worlds."

_____

_____

_____

_____

Feeling Two: "I need my work to have more meaning."

_____

_____

_____

_____

Feeling Three: "I need a clear picture of what being a Christian on the job looks like."

_____

_____

_____

_____

Feeling Four: "I need a faith that makes a difference in my life and my job."

_____

_____

_____

_____

Feeling Five: "I feel like I am not receiving any help to bring my two worlds together."

_____

_____

_____

_____

Rank those five feelings in order of your personal struggle.

3. John 17:15, 16 says, "My prayer is not that you take them out of the world but that you protect them from the evil one. They are not of the world, even as I am not of it" (NIV). How are we to apply this Scripture to our lives? How are we to be "in the world" but not "of the world"?

_____

_____

_____

_____

_____

4. In what ways has the church supported/not supported the idea of integrating our faith and our work?

_____

_____

_____

_____

5. What are your three biggest needs in learning how to allow your faith to shape your work?

   a. _____

   b. _____

   c. _____

6. Name a few ways that your faith aids you in "surviving" your work.

   _____

   _____

   _____

   _____

7. People of faith must learn to be comfortable, valuable, and intentional in two worlds. In these two arenas rage all of the battles of the heart. Between them are caught most of the big issues of life.

   What is your biggest hurdle in feeling comfortable, valuable, and intentional in your merger of faith and work?

   1) Comfortable (living seamlessly in both worlds)—

   _____

   _____

2) Valuable (making a contribution in your work and your faith)—

_____

_____

3) Intentional (being targeted in your involvement in kingdom and commerce)—

_____

_____

CHAPTER 2

WORKING IN
PARADISE

"OPPORTUNITY IS MISSED BY MOST PEOPLE BECAUSE IT
IS DRESSED IN OVERALLS AND LOOKS LIKE WORK."

—THOMAS A. EDISON

❋ Driving Thought

The exploration of Life@Work leads to a striking conclusion: Work was designed to allow us a deep participation in the life and work of God Himself.

❋ Drilling Down

When you think of the word *paradise,* what comes to mind?

Perhaps you see yourself sitting on a beach, cold drink in hand, sun on your face, breeze in your hair, a good book in your lap and turquoise-blue waters as far as the eye can see.

Or maybe you're lying under the stars in the Rockies, a spring-fed river running nearby with tomorrow's trout, your family asleep, a campfire popping with flames as lazy and silver-orange as the full moon.

Or how about this one? It's Monday morning and you're behind a desk. The phone is ringing, the computer's frozen and your assistant—if you are lucky enough to have one—is asking for time off as papers spill onto the floor. Your boss, meanwhile, walks by and reminds you that he wants to see your presentation in exactly fifty-seven minutes and thirty-three seconds.

For most of us, work and paradise are as related as bobsledding and Jamaica. They are antonyms, buzzing with the opposing energy of an oxymoron: freezer burn, jumbo shrimp, and working paradise. In fact, most of the cultural perceptions of paradise are marked by the *absence* of work: travel brochures, retirement magazines, and lottery advertisements. We are led to believe that work is at best a chore, a duty, or a way to pay the bills.

But that's not the way God designed it. Amazingly, He designed it as a deep participation in the life and work of God Himself. The purpose was to "take care" of the earth, to steward it. Indeed, man's continued stewardship is the linchpin of understanding a theology of work.

That does not mean, of course, that every workday feels like "paradise." We still deal with the thorns that have grown since man's Fall in the Garden. Even the most energized Life@Work has tough Tuesdays and frenetic Fridays.

If human society is a garden, then there are four institutions that must be nurtured for holistic health. From the earliest scenes of creation, we see God designing these four separate structures for people to explore life: Family, government, church, and work. Yes, God created *work* for us to explore, discover, and cultivate for His glory.

Mysteriously, a silence often surrounds the God-ordained institution of work, leaving modern explorers disoriented and puzzled.

"God has created me to do him some definite service," the Catholic thinker, John Henry Newman wrote, "he has committed some work to me which he has not committed to another."

If that is true, then why does the church say so little about it?

MAKING EVALUATION

Because this territory has been so long neglected, it in many ways is now an overgrown wilderness. The journey toward an effective, fulfilling Life@Work is not for the weak-kneed and fainthearted. It can be an unforgiving terrain. Unfortunately, the traditional sources for faith-based answers to life's dilemmas often fail to help. When mentioned at all, work generally is viewed as negative, something that keeps us from spending our time and energy on truly *important* issues—family and church. Thus, Life@Work typically finds itself shackled by the chains of misconceptions.

Consider these commonly held myths connected to work:

MYTH 1: WORK IS A FOUR-LETTER WORD. Ronald Reagan once said, "It's true, hard work never killed anybody, but I figure, why take the chance?" He was joking (we think). But it summarizes the conventional thinking that work is a necessary evil to the comforts of the American Dream. We grudgingly put in our time so that we can collect at the end of the month. The prize is all the rewards our consumer economy has to sell us.

The Christian spiritualized version of this popular attitude sees work as punishment that God delivered in anger after Adam and Eve directly disobeyed Him in the Garden of Eden. Work is a career-long punishment that all of us—past, present, and future—must endure because Adam and Eve bought into Satan's great lie.

The truth is that work was one of God's first assignments for Adam. God already had ordained work before the Fall. Genesis 2:15 reads, "The LORD

God took the man and put him in the Garden of Eden to *work it and take care of it*" (NIV, *emphasis added*). The time frame is critical. That was chapter two. Sin doesn't enter in until chapter three. Work is not a result of sin. Work was part of God's original creation. Like the family, work is "a creation ordinance"—a potential blessing and a divine assignment.

MYTH 2: WORK IS ENEMY TERRITORY. According to this presupposition, work is worldly. It is part of the secular system. "God stuff" includes such things as prayer, Bible study, worship services, and our donations of time and money to worthy "ministries."

This dichotomy—this split between the sacred and the secular—does not occur in God's Word. In fact, Scripture spends a good deal of ink and paper making the point that these two should be tied together—that work is part of God's everyday involvement with people.

MYTH 3: WORK IS SALVATION. For people who buy into this myth, work becomes God. They don't go to work; they go to Work. They don't seek success; they seek Success. They don't have ambition; they have Ambition. Their entire identity becomes wrapped up in their job.

This is a particularly dangerous side of the popular "work is the family" culture. Many organizations, religious or otherwise, sell a family-styled corporate culture as a benefit. People who take this idea to the extreme, however, can become emotional and spiritual prisoners to their jobs. The truth is that work is a great environment in which to discover God and to glorify God, but it is *not* God.

MYTH 4: WORK IS THE LAST PRIORITY. Teddy Roosevelt said, "Far and away the best prize that life offers is the chance to work hard at work worth doing." But many people make work their last priority, implying that it is not worth doing. The fact is an integrated holistic view of life *includes* work. God offers us the prize of a work that's worth doing, even if the church does not.

Consider a new set of priorities for life: God. That's it. There is no number two or number three or number four. In living out a life commitment to that priority, we must make Him an integrated part of everything we do—family, self, and work. He becomes the center of the flow and the source of alignment of all the parts of our life.

MYTH 5: WORK THAT IS ANOINTED ALWAYS SPELLS SUCCESS. Stories of skillful men and women who zoom up the career ladder of success fill the pages of everything from the Bible to *The Wall Street Journal.* It makes sense when we see skill and success partnering with each other.

But then there are other accounts, stories that also appear in Scripture and in the lives of men and women we all know: people of genuine skill who do not live in the glow of a successful career. They work hard and well, yet little career good happens. We need to make one important point as we begin our study of Life@Work: A God-filled work life does not always equate with career success. Unfortunately, many messengers offer that as the bait for folks to become more serious in pursuing a meaningful Life@Work. This study is not about unlocking worldly success, but God's key to unlocking His intended design for our work, whatever its circumstances or outcomes.

⊛ TAKING ACTION

1. How would you describe your concept of a day in paradise?
   Location—where would you be?

   _____

   _____

Participants—who would you be with?

_____

_____

Activity—how would you spend your time?

_____

_____

Weather—what would it feel like?

_____

_____

Food and Drink—what would you feast on?

_____

_____

2. Why would work be excluded from most people's answer to the above?

_____

_____

3. In what ways have Christians proposed that work is a curse?

_____

_____

_____

_____

4. How is work viewed in relation to the church and family by most Christians?

_____

_____

_____

_____

5. In Genesis 2:15 we see that work was assigned by the Lord before Adam's sin and thus before the curse. If work is a part of God's design of paradise, how does that change the theology of work believed by most Christians?

_____

_____

_____

_____

6. Why are the following statements myths?
   1) Work is a four-letter word.

_____

_____

   2) Work is enemy territory.

_____

_____

   3) Work is salvation.

_____

_____

4) Work is the last priority.

_____

_____

5) Work that is anointed always spells success.

_____

_____

7. Name one of the above mentioned "myths" that you have believed and allowed to guide your thoughts and actions in the last year.
Describe the effect this believed myth had on your life:

_____

_____

_____

8. Establishing priorities is a key to living a healthy life. Which of the following graphs best describes your life over the last few years?

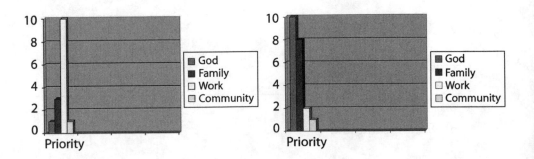

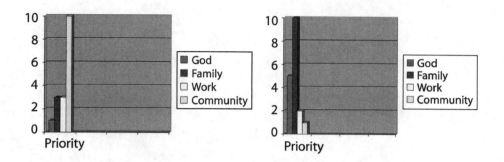

9. How can we have God at the hub of all of our concerns and priorities instead of a first, second, third approach?

_____

_____

_____

FOUR TOOLS FOR A POWERFUL LIFE@WORK

When I first began my search for a model from Scripture that frames the image of actively engaging in both the commercial and the kingdom sides of life, I inevitably kept coming back to David. The shepherd-king's life was so significant in the history of redemption that it stretched across several books of the Old Testament and gets mentioned a number of times in the New Testament, as well.

Conventional business wisdom today says find a mentor for your work who can pull you up to where you want to go. David's life has pull. He did what we all want to do: He lived a successful life. In Acts 13, God says of him, "David was a man after God's own heart and that after he accomplished all that God purposed for him, David passed on off the scene."

That is a pretty good eulogy.

What could be the ingredients behind such a mission-accomplished life? In Psalm 78 we get a telling snapshot into the work life and career of David.

This passage reveals four characteristics that contributed to the success of King David's Life@Work: David's calling, David's service, David's character, and David's skill.

> He chose David—*That is Calling*—his servant—*That is Service*—and took him from the sheep pens; from tending the sheep he brought him to be the shepherd of his people Jacob, of Israel his inheritance. And David shepherded them with integrity of heart—*That is Character*. With skillful hands he led them—*That is skill* (Ps. 78:70–72 NIV).

Calling, Service, Character, and Skill factors are not just unique to David, but are timeless and apply to any work context. They are four quiet yet powerful essentials for every man or woman to carry into their work setting. Each is a crucial intersection where faith must be intentionally employed to form our work.

Calling is our understanding of our divine job assignments. Skill is the unique set of abilities God gave us to fulfill our callings. Serving is the fundamental posture of our work toward others. Character is what binds it all together, the vital necessity of integrity and consistency of all of we are in all that we do.

The rest of this book will focus in more detail on those four tools and how you can incorporate them into your Life@Work.

SKILL@WORK

PEOPLE OF FAITH OUGHT TO *DELIVER*

SKILL IN THEIR WORK.

A good friend of mine loves to watch the Saturday afternoon show *The Yankee Woodshop.* He is an amazing carpenter and could very well host the show. It is astonishing to see a pile of lumber turned into an heirloom mahogany china cabinet in just under thirty minutes on the show. On one episode someone asked the master cabinetmaker on the show how long it takes to learn how to do that. He said, "Any ten year old could do it—with twenty years of experience."

The same is true for excellence in our on-the-job skills. We all would like to be the best at what we do, but few are willing to do what it takes to get there. Faith, however, calls us to the highest standard in all aspects of our life and work. Scripture has a great deal to say about skill, but for some reason we do not hear much about it. It is ironic that Jesus was a craftsman, yet skill is rarely associated with Christian faith.

Sadly, the result too often is that churchgoers have a reputation around the office as nice, honest people, but are not considered in the top of job rankings. To the contrary, Scripture challenges followers of Christ to raise the bar in their work, not lower the curve.

SKILL

*is understanding something completely
and transforming that knowledge
into creations of wonder and excellence.*

CHAPTER 3

SKILL IS IMPORTANT TO GOD

"'Tis God gives skill, but not without men's hand.
He could not make Antonio Stradivarius's violins
without Antonio."

—George Eliot,
a.k.a. Mary Ann Evans
(1819–1880)

⊛ Driving Thought

Skill is not just a business necessity but a spiritual imperative.

⊛ Drilling Down

Landing a Boeing 747 in Hong Kong once was one of the ultimate tests of an airline pilot's skill. Surrounded on three sides by water, the old Kai Tak Airport was as close as you could get in commercial aviation to making an aircraft-carrier landing. Only it was worse—carriers aren't surrounded by mountains. No other final approach in the world was as hairy as Kai Tak's.

As you flew in, you saw why. Out the windows was Hong Kong's urban mass of high-rise buildings wedged on a small sliver of land between the surrounding peaks and the South China Sea. Like grass in a concrete crack, Hong Kong, with its six-and-a-half million people, had nowhere to grow but straight up.

Dense blocks of apartment buildings stretched almost to the very edge of the airport tarmac. Boxed in by the city, Hong Kong had to reclaim land from the ocean to make the runway long enough for large airplanes, so it extended eleven thousand feet into the harbor. A range of precipitous peaks with steep slopes surrounded Hong Kong like a bowl.

Landing in that bowl, a plane had to drop from 1,800 to 675 feet in two minutes. The landing gear down and the flaps extended, it typically looked like the plane would crash straight into a mountain. All of sudden, the pilot banked into a thirty degree hard turn spiraling down. If you were on the right side of the airplane, you found yourself looking directly into apartment windows.

In the final thirty seconds of flight, the pilot had to level out the airplane, center it on the runway, touch down and stop its careening 540,000 pounds before it ran into Victoria Harbor.

Growing up in Hong Kong, I lived two miles from the end of the Kai Tak runway, directly under the flight path. Landing lights for the final approach were on the roof of the apartment building next to ours. It was against the law to fly kites because they could get tangled in the landing gear.

It was an awesome thing to see, hear, and feel those huge jets thunder overhead, just a few hundred feet off the ground. One right after another, they came in only minutes apart. No matter how many thousands I had already seen, I always had to watch the next one.

Skill in action is a wonderful thing to behold.

As we reflect on this core aspect of our work, we begin to ask a different set of questions: What does it mean to have skill, to be exceptionally good at something? How does one become a "standout performer" in a given task? We love to see skill in action, but what is it exactly? What is skill, really?

MAKING EVALUATION

Christopher Zeeman defined technical skill as "mastery of complexity." Our skill set is our competencies. The category of skill, however, involves more than masterful execution. If skill is just what we can do, then what sets us apart is the degree to which we can do it better than others. As a result, skill in our culture too often ends up as a competitive weapon of destruction. It is what enables us to beat out the person at the desk next to us.

Today's corporate culture is "Exhibit A" of skill run amuck. It is the dysfunctional dynamic of social Darwinism: the survival of the fittest. We sharpen the edges of our skill to fend off the other job applicants. We brandish our prowess to establish dominance before the next promotion comes around. We humiliate the competition, closing the deal right out from under them. Skill is the cunning that enables us to get away with as much as possible without getting caught.

This amoral outlook was the skill mentality of Goliath, the Philistine giant who defied the Army of Israel until David killed him with a slingshot and a stone. Goliath warred based on brute strength. Goliath audaciously challenged all comers, and he relied on his physical supremacy to win.

To a Goliath, skill is a zero sum game. There is a winner and there is a loser. If I am successfully skilled, it means you are not. If you are successfully skilled it means I am not. If I can beat you, then you have to serve under me. If you can beat me, then I have to serve under you.

This concept of skill has changed little since the beginning of time. What once was measured in scalps is today measured in pay stubs, client accounts, and corporate takeovers.

Whether we spend the week on the factory line or in the front office, work for many of us is a never-ending fight to the top of the pile. David Sarnoff was not far from the truth when he said, "Competition brings out the best in products and the worst in people." Those who make it to the top last only long enough to become the target of the next challenger on the way up.

These warriors of business survival do not build people, they beat people. It is raw, pagan savagery, only played out on a more civilized field of business.

Clearly, skill is a sail that needs a rudder. Thomas Merton was dead on when he said, "Unless we develop a moral, spiritual, and political wisdom that is proportionate to our technological skill, our skill may end us." This last decade of corporate America's legacy as an era of corruption only punctuates that fact.

The biblical picture of skill is quite different. God created skill to be a mastery that at its heart is constructive and creative. It is the weapon not of unhealthy competition, but of commitment to the welfare of others. It was Ralph Waldo Emerson who said, "Talent for talent's sake is a bauble and a show. Talent working with joy in the cause of universal truth lifts the possessor to new power as a benefactor."

It is not competition itself that is bad. Competition is the foundation of both democracy and capitalism. Both use competition to maximize the common good.

The faith perspective of work does not eliminate competition. To the contrary, Charlie is a competitor. He plays at the top of his game. He does his best. He drives for the best price. He seeks to make his business the best it can be. He does not do so, however, as a Goliath. No, he does so as a David, someone who passionately pursues his calling in harmony with the goodness of God. Goliath used his brute to decimate nations. David used his talents to build a nation.

The Old Testament word for skill comes directly from the Hebrew word *to know*. This is not just a superficial understanding of something, but to know completely and thoroughly. It is the same word, for instance, used to describe sexual intimacy between a husband and a wife.

The biblical definition of skill goes beyond mere knowledge—comprehensive as it may be. In addition to knowing something completely, skill also implies the capacity to translate knowledge into something of great value. As Leo F. Buscaglia said, "Your talent is God's gift to you. What you do with it is your gift back to God."

According to Scripture, skill is *knowing*, combined with the ability to *do*. It is *deep knowledge* in sync with *fine accomplishment*. Skill is the *best theory* blended with *unsurpassed practice*. When we operate with genuine biblical skill in our jobs and careers people are literally taken aback. Even when they are not sure how to explain what just happened, they sit up and take notice. Skill for followers of Christ is of that wondrous variety.

✸ TAKING ACTION

1. Skill in action is awe-inspiring. Name someone who has exhibited skill in such a way that you have been amazed by his/her performance, i.e. Tiger Woods' skill with a golf club . . .

   _____

2. Skill has been defined as "doing a common thing in an uncommon way." How does this definition differ or affirm from your previous thoughts on skill?

   _____

_____

_____

3. Contrast David and Goliath's representation of skill:

Goliath

_____

_____

David

_____

_____

4. Skill is a sail that needs a rudder. What is the rudder that determines whether skill is used to build or destroy?

_____

_____

_____

5. According to Scripture, skill is _knowing_, combined with the ability to _do_. It is _deep knowledge_ in sync with _fine accomplishment_. Skill is the _best theory_ blended with _unsurpassed practice_. If skill is the ability to both _know_ and _do_ in such a way that people take notice, how can this bring glory to God?

_____

_____

_____

6. A biblical concept of skill involves both creation and contribution. How do both of these concepts apply to your Life@Work?

_____

_____

_____

_____

7. Why does excellence matter to God?

_____

_____

8. One man defined excellence as "doing the best you can, where you are at, with what you have . . ." How can you live out this standard of excellence at your work?

_____

_____

9. In your area of skill, which part of the skill equation needs greater intensity, the knowing side or the doing side?

_____

_____

_____

10. What would be your top three skills?

   a. _____

   b. _____

   c. _____

CHAPTER 4

God Is
Important
to Skill

"I DO NOTHING APART FROM MY FATHER."

—A CARPENTER FROM NAZARETH

✹ DRIVING THOUGHT

A God-centered Life@Work delivers a skill that causes awe among humans and praise toward God.

✹ DRILLING DOWN

One of the bizarre cross-cultural experiences for a Westerner traveling to Eastern Europe during the rule of communism was to visit Soviet-style department stores. The most famous of them, the huge GUM mega-department store, was just off Red Square in Moscow.

Pronounced "goom" by the Russians, this large, gray mini-mall took up an entire city block. The street-level window displays included the typical mannequins standing in their rigamortis poses, fully dressed and accessorized. The colors, however, were a little off—too muted. They looked faded by the sun, but they were made that way. The style of the clothes were dated, like something you'd see in a fifteen-year-old rerun on

T.V. It was like walking through a time warp and entering a retro experience.

Inside were the typical departments: domestics, hardware, shoes, fashions, etc. Unlike in America, however, all the merchandise was behind counters, vigilantly manned by fire-plug shaped *"babushkas."* These older Russian women had the physical presence of NFL defensive linemen. If you dared touch something, they'd run at you with arms flailing, all the while screaming Russian invectives at your audacity to violate their domain. You never make that mistake twice—take it from me.

The sporting goods section was in the back of the store, accessible by the escalators. But in this store, shoppers randomly went up and down on either of the pair of escalators. That's because Soviet escalators rarely moved.

In a multi-story shopping megaplex, the escalators weren't much more than a fancy set of metal stairs. As a means for getting from one floor to another, an escalator still functions—with or without a working motor. It's much more productive, however, when fully powered and operating as its designer intended.

The same is true of skill.

Everyone has God-given skill. Talents and abilities are given to believers and unbelievers alike. Furthermore, skills function even when disconnected from their maker. That does not mean, however, that their maker is irrelevant to their use. To the contrary, just as skill is important to God, so too is God vitally important to skill.

Skill without God never reaches its full potential. It very well may be a resounding success in worldly terms, but its work will never have the spiritual substance for which it was made. For followers of Christ, implementing skill includes an additional dimension that is unavailable to men and women who chose to do life on their own. Besides the God-given ability born in us all, God comes alongside His disciples to actively sharpen and multiply the application of their skills. God is important to skill.

A God-centered Life@Work delivers skill in a way that's distinct from non-believers. A life fully integrating its faith with its work will involve God in the use of its skills. As the examples of Scripture show, when we bring God into our Monday through Friday lives, the testimony of our work will increasingly have God's fingerprints on it.

MAKING EVALUATION

David's debut on the public stage was so stunning a display of skill that the young shepherd was transformed instantly into the warrior legend of a nation. The David and Goliath epic is a familiar story of a scornful bully, his pagan provocation to God's good name, the hand-wringing inaction of God's people, and the spontaneous initiative of a dark-horse challenger. The turning point in the drama, however, was David's skill in delivering a small stone to just the right location on Goliath's temple with sufficient velocity to cause the man-giant to fall with a thud.

You may ask, what does God have to do with it? Any farm boy worth his salt can throw a rock. Who needs God to do that? You might be right . . . if you had all day . . . and a pile full of rocks . . . and if he would just stand there until you hit him in the right spot. On the other hand, if you have just one rock and you want to kill a murderous giant *and* live to tell about it . . . well, in that case, you'd better pray.

You know the story. The people of Israel spent days cowered "dismayed and terrified" (1 Sam. 17:11 NIV). When Goliath came out each day, "they all ran from him in great fear" (1 Sam. 17:24 NIV). Yet, the crisis was over in an instant. Goliath lost his head, David was a hero and the Israelites defeated the Philistines.

Almost lost in the drama is a short dialogue between Goliath and David, just before the Philistine went down. Up to this point all the talk had come from Goliath in the form of a taunting monologue: "This day I defy the ranks of Israel! Give me a man and let us fight each other." But in a unique battlefield speech, David breaks the conspicuous silence of the Israelites with a clear manifesto:

> You come against me with sword and spear and javelin, but I come against you in the name of the LORD Almighty, the God of the armies of Israel, whom you have defied. This day the LORD will hand you over to me, and I'll strike you down and cut off your head. Today I will give the carcasses of the Philistine army to the birds of the air and the beasts of the earth, and the whole world will know that there is a God in Israel. All those gathered here will know that it is not by sword or spear that the LORD saves; for the battle is the LORD's, and he will give all of you into our hands (1 Sam. 17:43–47 NIV).

Members of the surrounding battlefield audience no doubt had different responses to David's short address. Goliath balked when he saw someone of such low—aah, make that no—military caliber. The balance of the Philistine army was probably amused by the spectacle. David's brothers were mortified and embarrassed beyond words. Everyone else on their side likely held their breath or closed their eyes.

What Goliath viewed as a contest of skill between two soldiers, David understood as a partnership between the skilled action of an individual and God's power to make things happen. Along with his sling, David had an even more significant secret weapon: His dependence on God.

David's picture of how he saw God's role in his use of skill is clear from what he told Goliath. Goliath was on his own: "You come against me with sword and spear and javelin . . ." All Goliath has is his own physical capability and the tools of war. David had himself, his slingshot and *his God*: ". . . I come against you in the name of the LORD Almighty, the God of the armies of Israel." To David, God's role was crucial to the outcome of the battle. He continued, "The LORD will hand you over to me . . . and the whole world will know that there is a God in Israel." David carried a sling, but he put his trust in his God. He declared, "It is not by sword or spear that the LORD saves . . . the battle is the LORD'S, and he will give all of you into our hands."

Here in sum is David's "philosophy of skill" that Goliath, unfortunately, had very little time to ponder: "You have your stuff and I have my stuff. But besides that, I have God and you don't. Therefore you will die." Goliath had "skill" while David had "God-skill."

As followers of Christ, we have available to us all the power and wisdom of God Himself. God has given us the Holy Spirit to live and work in and through us. He wants to take our level of skill to heights otherwise impossible to reach. We must trust Him. It is up to us to ask for His help. Why climb the escalator on our own power? Call on its maker. Use it as He intended.

❈ TAKING ACTION

1. What was the difference between the resources that David and his enemy

Goliath brought to the table in their encounter?

_____

_____

2. How does the following statement affect your concept of skill?

Skill without God will never reach its full human potential. It may very well be a resounding success in worldly terms, but its work will never have the spiritual substance that it was made for.

_____

_____

3. Each one should use whatever gift he/she has received to serve others, faithfully administering God's grace in its various forms.

According to I Peter 4:10, God has given each believer a spiritual gift or "God empowered ability." Have you discovered this gift in your life? If so, what would you consider to be your gift? *(See the following passages for a list of gifts: Romans 12:6–8, 1 Corinthians 12:8–10, 28–30; Ephesians 4:11).*

_____

_____

4. We have spiritual gifts, and we also have talents that God built into us at birth. What is it that you do best? (Do you relate to people well? Are you creative? Are you good with your hands? Are you a leader? Do you excel at serving others?)

What is your earliest memory of this skill being used?

_____

_____

5. How can you integrate the working of the Holy Spirit into your Skill@Work, just as you would integrate Him into your spiritual gifts at church?

_____

_____

6. Can you relate to the escalator in the Russian department store?

_____

_____

Which of the following describes your Skill@Work (check one):

_____ Escalator reduced to stairs. You have skills, but use them without the empowerment of the Lord. Therefore, you miss out on a lot of potential.

_____ Escalator fully empowered. You have skills and are using them in dependence on the Lord. Your potential is being maximized.

7. Fill in the following prayer:

Lord, I pray that You would guide me in using my skill of _____ to make a contribution in _____ that would glorify God through _____ .

CHAPTER 5

DISCOVERING
YOUR GREATNESS

"WHAT I DO IS ME. FOR THIS I CAME."

—GERALD STANLEY HOPKINS

We will never experience the Life@Work that God intended for us until we answer the question, "What is my created greatness?"

⊛ DRILLING DOWN

Andrew Clemons was an improbable candidate for any type of hall of fame.

He was born in 1857 to a German family that had fled poverty in their motherland only to find that poverty stalking them as refugees here.

Life was hard on the family, and even harder for Andrew. At age five, he was struck with "Brain Fever"—what we now know as Encephalitis—and almost died. And even though he survived, the illness left him deaf in both ears. Eventually his speech atrophied and he became mute, as well.

His father found opportunity by opening a wagon shop in McGregor, Iowa, a Mississippi River town where pioneers bought the supplies they needed to continue their trek to the West.

Building wagons gave the Clemons family the toehold it needed in the New World. Perhaps now their children could grow up and make good. The dream they were working for seemed possible, except, of course for Andrew.

If immigrants had it hard on the eighteenth-century American frontier, those with physical disabilities had it even harder. A deaf and mute child had little future. Andrew seemed destined for a lifetime of dependence on others.

One day, however, Andrew was playing on the bluffs of Old Man River when he found an exposed cliff with beautiful, colored layers of sandstone. He put some of the sand in his pocket and took it home. Later he began playing with the sand, putting it in bottles and using the colors to make designs. People liked his colorful sand-filled bottles, and soon he was getting orders for so many that it became a full-time job. The more bottles he created, the better he became. Eventually he began creating detailed pictures: elaborate landscapes, ships and trains, even portraits. Clemens became famous for his work. He received orders from around the world. People came all the way from Europe just to watch him work.

Clemens had single-handedly invented a new art form: sand art. He used no paint, no brush, and no glue—only a few crude wooden instruments and naturally colored grains of sand.

To see one of the few surviving Andrew Clemens sand bottles is to behold a true marvel. They are exquisitely detailed. Their colors are true-to-life, with depth and light created by subtle shading. Perhaps most amazingly, they were made one grain of sand at a time.

In the end, Andrew Clemens' story is not about his limitations. Instead, it's the lesson of discovered and developed genius. Clemens worked with what God gave him: nimble hands, a creative mind, discarded bottles, and common sand from a nearby riverbank. These were his simple ingredients for making something of magnificence.

There was much Andrew Clemens couldn't do, but that didn't matter; he found the one thing he did better than anyone else. Ralph Waldo Emerson said, "Each man has his own vocation; his talent is his call. There is one direction in which all space is open to him." Clemens found the door with his name on it. And by going through it, he discovered a whole world of possibilities.

How do you do that? How do you figure out what God made you for? How can you find and develop your unique God-given gifts amid life's hard realities and despite your personal limitations? You will never experience the Life@Work that God intended you for until you answer the question, "What is my created greatness?"

MAKING EVALUATION

While there are many aspects to who we are as individuals, two factors are especially significant to discovering our "Sweet Spot." Our point of greatness is usually found at the intersections of what we are good at and what we like to do. Greatness requires both desire and knack. Aspiration without ability will get us nowhere. On the other hand, talent without motivation will never excel either. Greatness is an amalgam of both.

Discovering our greatness comes from maximizing the alignment between our shape and our job. When our skill set matches the critical skills of our job, we are in our work-world rhythm. To the degree that the task requirements in our jobs fall outside our core motivated abilities, we will experience depletion as we exert the extra effort necessary to work outside what we like to do. Burnout is the unintended consequence of someone who is poorly wired for his work.

If you are not good with numbers and you suddenly take on major financial accounting responsibilities, your job satisfaction will go down. If you are not good at selling and yet your job requires it, eventually you will find yourself emotionally depleted by working out of your weakness.

If, on the other hand, much of your wiring goes untapped by your job, you will end up bored. People who are bored at work typically seek an outlet for their passion through their avocation. When you see someone who spends just as much time with Little League as he does at work, chances are he is compensating for a bad job fit. Clubs, community boards and churches are full of volunteers who are seeking an outlet because of a bad fit at work.

Maximum job fit comes from discovering your greatness and working out of it. That is what David did. When David was slinging smooth stones toward Goliath's forehead, he was working out of his greatness and the Greatness of his God.

David's smooth execution in his sweet spot, however, did not come over night. The product of his life experiences prepared him. David was tested and prepared as a shepherd boy. In the fields working with sheep, he learned what he was good at, what he was not good at, what he liked, and what he did not like. Furthermore, he practiced and honed his skills. David was able to kill Goliath because he had already passed the tests of killing a bear and a lion.

Peter Drucker was dead on when he said we ought to build our lives on our islands of strength. To do that, we have to know what we're great at. John Gardner explained that, "Mastery is not something that strikes in an instant, like a thunderbolt, but a gathering power that moves steadily through time, like weather." The key to not drowning in the ocean of possibilities is mapping the limits of the shoreline of our capabilities.

The obvious place to start is with what we are good at. Discovering what we are good at takes some thought. What you are looking for is not one answer like "I am good at sales." Rather you are looking for all the things that make you good at sales: communication, networking, relating to people, etc. These are all clues. They paint a picture. That picture is not a specific job but a composite portrait of a skill set.

Being good at something is not enough to propel us to greatness. It requires an accompanying passion. Bob Biehl says that when you get down to it, people do what they *want* to do. It takes "want-to." What do you want to do? Biehl is right: If we are doing what we want to do, we will arrive early and stay late. On the other hand, if our job is something we don't want to do, we will show up late and leave early. We can't overlook our gut desires. They are part of our God-given wiring just as much as our talents and abilities.

❋ TAKING ACTION

1. Describe the concept of "created greatness."

   _____

   _____

2. What do the following verses from Psalm 139 say about our design?

   "For you created my inmost being; you knit me together in my mother's womb. I praise you because I am fearfully and wonderfully made; your works are wonderful, I know that full well" (Ps. 139:13, 14 NIV).

3. What is your created greatness? How were you "fearfully and wonderfully made?" What did God have in mind when He knit you together?

_____

_____

_____

4. David knew he could never do what God wanted him to do wearing someone else's armor. That was not him. It was only as he gave himself the freedom to be what God had made him that he found his greatness. Can you relate to David's plight of casting off the armor of another to become who God designed him to be?

_____

_____

_____

5. Our point of greatness is usually found at the intersections of what we are good at and what we like to do.

What skill area has brought you the greatest and most consistent success?

_____

_____

_____

What do you passionately like to do? What energizes you most?

_____

_____

_____

6. Do some reverse engineering by looking at your history . . .

   In the space provided below list every job that you have ever had. Read back over the list and think through each position. What did you learn about yourself from each one? What did you do in that job that you were really good at? Finally, ask yourself what you were asked to do that you were bad at? Write any weaknesses that these episodes revealed in a third column.

Job	Things you were good at . . .	Things you were bad at . . .
Example:		
Camp Counselor	*Relationships*	*Discipline/confrontation*
_____	_____	_____
_____	_____	_____
_____	_____	_____
_____	_____	_____

Now write a few words summarizing your list:
"I like working at" . . .

_____

_____

"I am good at" . . .

_____

_____

"I know that I am not good at" . . .

_____

_____

As you fill in the blanks from your experience a general picture will emerge. Your history will demonstrate a pattern. That pattern is your skill set. It is the unique package of assets that God has given you.

SECTION 2

CALLING@WORK

PEOPLE OF FAITH OUGHT TO *EXPERIENCE*

CALLING IN THEIR WORK.

Calling, in its fullness, is an idea too good to be true, unless and until Jesus is involved in the conversation. When He calls, He does so with great precision. Not only does He know what needs to be accomplished and how those tasks fit within eternal boundaries, He also knows the one He is calling. He made that person specifically to do what they are being called to do. Like a giant job match service in the sky, Jesus pairs His children with His kingdom tasks.

Jesus will not ask us to do something for which we are not equipped. Why would He create us improperly to accomplish a career job for which we are unsuited and unprepared? Jesus does ask us sometimes to do tasks that are not much fun. Daniel was supremely prepared to be the top administrator to multiple kings. They were cruel pagans, and he was prisoner in a foreign land. All things considered, he probably would have preferred to trade some position for some freedom.

Calling need not be a lifetime mystery. God intended from the beginning to unfold His plans and desires for each us with specificity. If there is anything that ought to sound good in today's world it is this: Work can have eternal purpose, and our lives can have fullness of meaning through the work we do.

CALLING

is God's personal invitation
for me to work on His agenda,
using the talents I have been given
in ways that are eternally significant.

CHAPTER 6

CALLED BY WHOM AND ABOUT WHAT?

"YOU ARE NOT HERE MERELY TO MAKE A LIVING . . . YOU ARE HERE TO ENRICH THE WORLD, AND YOU IMPOVERISH YOURSELF IF YOU FORGET THE ERRAND."

—WOODROW WILSON

⚙ DRIVING THOUGHT

In the transitory swirling currents of the temporary, calling moors us to the eternal.

⚙ DRILLING DOWN

A woman in the back left corner of the room raised her hand and asked a question that brought silence to the crowd. Side conversations stopped. People who had been writing put down their pens and looked up from their papers. Those who had been anticipating the end of this Q&A session took a break from loading their briefcases.

The woman had asked out loud a question that many of them had asked in their hearts.

"So, how do you know when you are called to your job?" she had said. And that's all it took to quite the masses.

"I mean, is there any way to really be sure that you are doing the most fulfilling thing possible?"

This was not a church meeting. It was not a ministry retreat. It was not a Christian conference. This was a room full of design engineers who worked all around the world for the Big Three auto companies.

The question peeked their interests because it's universal. We all have a sense that there is something specific we ought to do with our lives, and we don't want to miss that destiny.

It wasn't an easy question to answer, at least not in this setting. How do you explain a biblical concept to such a diverse audience? Calling is a God term. It comes straight from Scripture. It is a word Jesus uses to describe how He communicates with His followers regarding what they will do in life. To be "called," we have to know God and listen when He talks.

When secular business magazines feature stories on calling, however, there is a limited amount of help they can offer. We don't determine our calling by holding personal intellectual summits. We determine our calling by listening to our God coach us through the work path He wants us to take.

Calling, at its most basic level, is the expression of a higher purpose. In the transitory swirling currents of the temporary, calling moors us to the eternal. Beyond God, we cannot be moved. Calling constantly reminds us that our lives are larger than our puny selves.

In the Bible, calling is twofold: God calls each person to Himself (to salvation), and God calls each person to his or her work as part of God's divine agenda. Calling, then, is both general and specific. Our calling in life, in the words of Os Guinness, means that "everything we are, everything we do, and everything we have is invested with a special devotion, dynamism, and direction lived out as a response to His summons and service." Our first calling is to a relationship with Him; yet, that relationship is pursued in the context of a second subsequent calling, the work that He created us to do out of our love for Him. Neglecting either calling is a mistake.

God calls each of us to a specific work assignment. When Paul was speaking to philosophers in Athens, he made it clear that God has a very precise plan for individual lives: "From one man he made every nation of men, that they should inhabit the whole earth; and *he determined the times set for them and the exact places where they should live*" (Acts 17:26; NIV *emphasis added*). God designed *me* to do something for *Him*.

We are men and women who do consulting, banking, truck driving, plumbing, doctoring, full-time parenting, teaching, pastoring and a host of other things. God calls individuals to all kinds of careers. The factor we all share, however, is the One who has called us.

Anchored in eternal reality, we are freed to view our work from a perspective above the constantly changing of day-to-day business. At the same time, we are not "above it all," exempted from or unchallenged by the ever-changing realities of the work world before us, temporary as that work may be. God throws us into the fray, and our work involves the implementation of God's agenda in history.

When we come to grips with the idea and magnitude of God's calling, we are less tempted to define success as a promotion to the seventeenth floor or a vacation in the Swiss Alps. In our work we are called to higher, more attainable realities and to a deeper fulfillment and sustaining significance.

MAKING EVALUATION

The biblical concept of calling, however, is confusing if we do not understand the difference and connection between calling, purpose, and meaning. They are not the same things, but they are closely connected.

1. PURPOSE

Purpose in Scripture is synonymous with God's sovereign design, His overarching view of history. It is what He is accomplishing. Our work is not some arbitrary and random choice that does not make any difference. Its primary objective is not only to put food on the table and provide a comfortable retirement. Sure, the bills must be paid, but there's more to work than survival. Our individual, personal, just-for-me work calling is part of God's larger agenda in history. We actually have a part in God's plan.

We are to serve God's purpose, whatever it is. Very few men in the Bible knew exactly what God's purpose was during their lifetime. Some of the prophets did, at least to some extent. We know God's purpose only if He chooses to reveal it to us.

Even though we do not necessarily know all the details, here's what we do know:

- God operates off of a master plan, even though He does not always tell us what it is.
- God specifically fits each of us as Christians into the larger workings of His overall plan.
- We serve His purpose through faith by following our best understanding of His calling on our lives.

As Christians, we know our work has purpose because we are serving a God whose purpose is bigger than us. To look up into the night sky at the end of the day and know that our work and life are part of His bigger plan supplies an inner joy and satisfaction that can come from nothing else.

2. CALLING

If purpose is something we serve, calling is something we discern. Calling is what we do individually to fit into God's purpose. Because we are "called according to His purpose," it is imperative that we discover exactly what our calling is. According to Ephesians: "In him we were also chosen [or called], having been predestined according to the plan of him who works out everything in conformity with the purpose of his will" (Eph. 1:11 NIV). God calls us to serve in a way that is consistent with how He has designed us. Finding our calling is about learning how God has designed us to serve Him.

3. MEANING

God's purpose is something we serve. Our calling is something we know. Meaning is something we are to enjoy. If we are accurately living out our calling, we will experience the incredible sense of meaning from our work that only God can provide. Meaning is a fruit. It is the peace and satisfaction of knowing our work is in concert with God's plans.

If we don't have personal relationships with God, then our careers don't have nearly the sense of meaning that is available to a Christian. We may be single-minded and mission-driven in what we do, but our work is necessarily a task force of one. It is all about me. I do the same work, but I do not receive the same enjoyment, the same meaning, the same satisfaction. I lack the meaning of my work being part of something larger than myself. We are to serve purpose. We are to know calling. We are to enjoy meaning. All three are work specific and God specific.

✹ TAKING ACTION

1. Describe the concept of calling as written of in this chapter.

_____

_____

_____

2. What are the two types of calling in scripture? How do they differ?

_____

_____

_____

3. In what ways have you experienced these callings?

_____

_____

_____

4. What do the following passages have to say about our calling?

_____

_____

_____

Matthew 28:19, 20 (NIV)

"Therefore go and make disciples of all nations, baptizing them in the name of the Father and of the Son and of the Holy Spirit, and teaching them to obey everything I have commanded you. And surely I am with you always, to the very end of the age."

Acts 1:8 (NIV)

"But you will receive power when the Holy Spirit comes on you; and you will be my witnesses in Jerusalem, and in all Judea and Samaria, and to the ends of the earth."

Matthew 5:13, 14 (NIV)

"You are the salt of the earth. But if the salt loses its saltiness, how can it be made salty again? It is no longer good for anything, except to be thrown out and trampled by men. You are the light of the world. A city on a hill cannot be hidden."

5. According to the chapter, what is the difference in the following terms?

Purpose: _____

_____

Calling: _____

_____

Meaning: _____

_____

6. In what ways have you observed the following three traps in your life or the life of someone around you?

Trap one
Allowing work to drive you.
We should be driven by our God-given calling and not let the demands of our job set our priorities.

_____

_____

Trap two
Asking work to supply your identity.
Our identity is to be found in our relationship in Christ not our job titles.

_____

_____

Trap three
Using work to ignore your family.
A calling to work does not take away from our privileges, obligations, joys, and pleasures of home life.

_____

_____

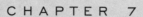

CHAPTER 7

CALLED BY NAME

"It is men who wait to be selected, and not those who seek, from whom we may expect the most efficient service."

—Ulysses S. Grant

❀ DRIVING THOUGHT

God calls us to our Life@Work—and sometimes He does it so we can hear Him.

❀ DRILLING DOWN

The man was just doing his job. Someone had to, and he was intensely task-focused in his work. His position description probably read something like this: "Stop the threat. Thwart the competition." It was the kind of dirty work reserved for a potential star, someone earning his stripes. If he succeeded with this high-profile assignment, it would place him on the fast track.

In his profession, title and position meant everything. This was not the kind of organization where everybody's office was the same size or where whoever arrived first in the morning parked closest to the front door. Rank had its privileges.

Saul was a young Pharisee. He'd been given a job to do, and he was doing it.

It was no surprise that Saul was chosen to head the task force against the new threat labeled "Christian." Although such a plum opportunity of prosecuting heretics normally would have gone to a Pharisee with more tenure, Saul was so far in front of the rest of the crowd that it was clear he deserved the honor.

Going from town to town and using a network of synagogue informants, Saul systematically pounded on their doors and dragged them out to accountability. They were frightened and many were poor and unschooled. These people honestly believed Jesus was the Son of God.

He was just on his way to the next town—in this case Damascus—and the next group of heretics. This was his job 24/7, and he would not rest until it was finished. Acts 9 picks up the story:

> As he neared Damascus on his journey, suddenly a light from heaven flashed around him. He fell to the ground and heard a voice say to him, "Saul, Saul, why do you persecute me?"
>
> "Who are you, Lord?" Saul asked.
>
> "I am Jesus, whom you are persecuting," he replied. "Now get up and go into the city, and you will be told what you must do."
>
> The men traveling with Saul stood there speechless; they heard the sound but did not see anyone. Saul got up from the ground, but when he opened his eyes he could see nothing. So they led him by the hand into Damascus (Acts 9:3–8 NIV).

In an instant, Saul's life was changed. He made a 180-degree about-face. He went from murderous persecutor to believer. How could that be? What happened? The answer was simple. It was Jesus, the Person he had been trying to silence and snuff out.

For Paul, the calling to faith and to a career task came from Jesus simultaneously. He began a new life, and he never looked back.

MAKING EVALUATION

How do we know our calling? The most obvious method is exactly what "call" implies: hearing God talk to us directly. It might be an audible voice. It may be a dream, a portent or a vision. Whatever it is, we have been personally visited and spoken to by God. The message He gave is unambiguous. God called us by name. He communicated in person.

Indeed, that is one of the ways calling happens in Scripture. These events are often quite dramatic, like Samuel who was trying to sleep in the temple when he heard God calling his name, or Mary who was visited by an angel and informed that her calling was to be mother to the King of kings.

Of the ways God chooses to call men and women to career tasks, calling them by name happens less often in Scripture than the other two methods (which we'll talk about in upcoming chapters). Nevertheless, call by name He does.

How do we know if God is calling us by name? Consider these guidelines:

IT *MIGHT* BE CALLING BY NAME IF . . . I HEAR GOD SPEAK.

Barry Brown was attending a tent meeting when a force he couldn't describe compelled him to the altar during the invitation. The 15-year-old began to weep, which was not his nature. Very unexpectedly, he heard God speak and clearly tell him that his life-career was to be a pastor. No one else heard the communication, but its reality was seared in the man's memory.

From that day forward, Barry faithfully pursued his God-given call to be a pastor. He did not look back; nor did he have second thoughts. His movement has only been forward toward that finish line. He planted a vibrant fellowship in the city limits of San Francisco eighteen years ago, and he plans to die there helping Golden Gate Community Church grow.

When we encounter people who have been called by name, they seldom display career "unsettledness." They know what they are supposed to be doing, and they refer to the certainty of their call constantly in conversation and in personal reflection.

IT *MIGHT* BE CALLING BY NAME IF . . . GOD'S SPEAKING IS CONFIRMED BY OTHER MEANS.

When God calls you by name, it's seldom an isolated incident. Jesus came to visit Mary, the mother of Jesus, through an angel, but then confirmed that life work in subsequent conversation with Joseph. God called Gideon to a specific task and experienced confirmation through the famous fleece. Moses was stunned by the burning bush, but was then was handed a miracle-working staff that confirmed countless times over the next decades that God's call was real.

When God speaks to you in a personal and discernible way, it is a singular moment in time. As sure as that might make you of what He's calling you to do, He almost always follows up with additional indications of His original message.

IT'S PROBABLY *NOT* CALLING BY NAME IF . . . WHAT I HAVE HEARD GOD SPEAK BEFORE TURNED OUT NOT TO BE SO.

"God told me . . ." is not uncommon to hear among followers of Christ. Over time, it often turns out that either God was wrong or that the person heard something other than God. Since God is never wrong, . . . well, you get the picture.

Remember, such communication is almost always reserved for unique and special—even singular—occasions. It is a huge deal to receive such communication from God and a huge deal to claim it.

Some of the most caustic comments recorded in the Old Testament come from God's prophets to "peers" who claimed to be prophets, but who weren't. Their claims to have heard from God were false. The messages of those false prophets were proven wrong as events turned out differently than they predicted. We don't want to claim to have heard God speak, only to be proven wrong.

IT'S PROBABLY *NOT* CALLING BY NAME IF . . . I CAN'T CLEARLY IDENTIFY THE TIME OR PLACE OF COMMUNICATION.

People who hear from God are unanimous about this: they know what He said and when He said it. Just like with Moses, there is always a time and place associated with the experience of God's call. The same was true for Gideon (Judg. 6:11–14) and Mary (Luke 1:26–38) and for many others.

The pattern is obvious. When God calls someone by name and you ask Him to relate the experience, He can do so in living and moving color. It isn't fuzzy. If you think God has called you by name and you cannot recall the time or place, then you probably weren't called like you thought you were.

✸ TAKING ACTION

1. How do we know our calling?

   _____

   _____

   _____

   _____

2. What observations can you make from the calling of the following biblical characters?

   Paul (Saul)

   _____

   _____

   _____

   Moses

   _____

   _____

   _____

   Mary

   _____

   _____

   _____

Gideon

_____

_____

_____

3. What are some forms of communication the Lord uses to call us?

_____

_____

_____

4. One of the surest methods of being sure of our calling is being called by

_____.

5. How do you know if you have been called by name? React to the following statements and corresponding questions:

   It _might_ be calling by name if . . . I hear God speak. Do you feel a sense of certainty that God has communicated something specifically to you?

   _____

   _____

   _____

   It _might_ be calling by name if . . . God's speaking is confirmed by other means. In what other ways has God confirmed His specific calling to you?

   _____

_____

_____

It's probably *not* calling by name if . . . What I have heard God speak before turned out not to be so. Have you been wrong about God's calling before?

_____

_____

_____

It's probably *not* calling by name if . . . I can't clearly identify the time or place of communication. When, where, and how did God communicate your specific calling to you?

_____

_____

_____

6. Have you ever felt like God spoke to you? If so, how did He speak and how was it confirmed?

_____

_____

_____

7. Why does the concept of "God speaking to us" sometimes make us nervous?

_____

_____

_____

8. Do you know anyone who claims to have a "calling by name" experience? What is his/her story?

_____

_____

_____

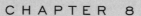

CHAPTER 8

CALLED BY DESIRE

"THE BEST CAREERS ADVICE TO GIVE TO THE YOUNG IS 'FIND OUT WHAT YOU LIKE DOING BEST AND GET SOMEONE TO PAY YOU FOR DOING IT.'"

—KATHARINE WHITEHORN

Desire is almost always found at the core of a calling.

⊛ DRILLING DOWN

Ernest Shakleton was an early twentieth-century polar explorer, but he isn't known for his discoveries. Instead, Shakleton left his mark with an epic story of persistence in the face of failure and almost certain death.

Shakelton's father was a doctor who pushed his son to medicine, but his young heart felt the pull of the oceans. On his first voyage, he rounded Cape Horn off the southern tip of Chile, looked over the rail to the South and felt drawn to the Antarctic. The dream of probing the globe's icy underbelly captivated him. He was agitated by explorer's wanderlust. At that point, no one had been to the earth's southernmost point.

You don't reach the South Pole in a day. Like any calling, it's a lifetime pursuit. So for twenty-four years, Shackleton worked at this calling, slowly climbing the maritime ranks in British merchant shipping. Action and preparation followed his desires.

His 1914 Antarctic expedition was his third, but he was not discouraged by previous failures or by the fact that someone had reached the South Pole ahead of him. Undeterred, he redefined his objective: Leading the first expedition across this forbidding uninhabited continent on foot. Calling always finds an opportunity of expressing itself.

On the day before Shackleton was to land his men on Antarctic, their ship became hopelessly locked within an earlier-than-usual ice pack. Ice crushed the ship and it sank, leaving the castaways on a frozen island destined to melt from underneath them. Shackleton realized his primary calling was not to a continent, but to captain an expedition of men, come what may.

The story of their subsequent ordeal is so impossibly grueling as to defy belief. They pushed, pulled, and sledged three lifeboats over six hundred miles of contorted ice. Fifteen months after they were marooned on the ice, they reached open water. They then sailed the lifeboats one hundred miles north to the nearest land, Elephant Island. But the island offered little hope of rescue and not much more than a piece of *terra firma* on which to die.

Shackleton chose five men and set out in one of the boats in search of South Georgia Island, the nearest human settlement. It was an eight-hundred-mile voyage across the earth's worst ocean in an open boat. They had to rely on readings from a sextant in a thrashing boat to plot their way. If they miss-navigated by even one degree, they would miss the tiny speck of land and sail into frozen oblivion.

Their eighteen-day voyage to South Georgia is considered one of the history's greatest feats of seamanship. Landfall, however, did not bring rescue.

Wind-bound on the uninhabited side of South Georgia, they had to cross the snow-covered mountainous island on foot.

With frostbitten hands and feet, ninety feet of rope and a carpenter's pick, they made a thirty-six hour climb that has been replicated only one other time—by elite British commandos outfitted with full modern alpine gear. Finally, on the afternoon of May 20, 1916, they walked into the Island's whaling port from which they originally departed for Antarctica. When they opened the door of the whaling headquarters, the director asked the men standing before him, "Who, the hell are you?" One of the unrecognizable skeletons staring at him replied, "My name is Shackleton."

Against all odds, Shackleton fulfilled his calling. He did not lose a single man. The name of his original ship proved prescient of his expedition's fate. It was the *Endurance*. How did Shackleton persist to success? He was just following the deep desire of his innate and lifelong calling to lead.

Making Evaluation

What looks like obsession from the outside is sometimes nothing less than the insatiable desire behind a calling. There is something that compels, drives, and pushes. It cannot be ignored or brushed aside. As the novelist Leo Rosten wrote of his own profession, "The only reason for being a professional writer is that you can't help it."

The requirement to go, or be, or do comes from a mysterious inner coercion that is invisible and often misunderstood—both by the individual who lives with it and those who watch it. To be "called by desire" is like having an internal gyroscope. Even if you lean the other direction, its centrifugal force pulls you pack toward its preferred axis. This sense of calling can be difficult to live with—and difficult to live without. How do you explain a force that is often neither logical nor observable? But, then again, how could you go on without it?

Identifying this calling is a process of definition, identifying both what you are and what you are not. To determine if a desire is not just a bad case of heartburn, but instead a genuine God-given direction, here are some questions—both positive and negative—to use as filters:

IT *MIGHT* BE CALLING BY DESIRE IF . . . THE SENSE OF URGENCY IS PERSISTENT AND RELATIVELY LONG-STANDING.

A calling is more than a passing fancy. Life always has zigs and zags. It's not a passion of the moment: two months ago your overwhelming urge was to open a retail business in the center of Chicago and today it is to become a professional athlete. No, a calling is an abiding passion of your soul. When God places a desire on your heart and then uses that desire to call you to do something specific, it usually is something that builds and is seasoned over time, not something that just shows up on our doorstep today for us to do tomorrow.

IT IS PROBABLY *NOT* CALLING BY DESIRE IF . . . I AM COMPLETELY UNEQUIPPED TO GET THE JOB DONE.

God equips whom He calls and calls whom He equips. If you feel called to do something that is outside the bounds of who God has made you, then it probably is not a calling.

Calling is more about doing than it is about thinking. Calling requires that you take action that results in accomplishing something. Many people have dreams they might equate with God's call; but calling is about doing, not dreaming. Dreaming is often part of the equation, but the dream must result in tangible motion.

IT IS PROBABLY *NOT* CALLING BY DESIRE IF . . . I QUIT WHEN I ENCOUNTER SIGNIFICANT HURDLES.

Robert Morrison was the first Protestant missionary in China, arriving in 1807 as a 25-year-old with a passion for the Chinese people to know Jesus. He died in China 27 years later a very discouraged man. He had baptized ten Chinese, and he considered his work a failure.

In fact, his influence stands as one of the most significant contributions to the Christian church in China of any person in the Chinese-speaking world. Why? Robert Morrison translated the Bible into Chinese, as well as compiling a six-volume Chinese dictionary. He made possible the huge influx of missionaries that followed. Tens of millions of Chinese have come to know Christ as a result of his lifelong effort.

Getting to China was hard enough for Morrison, but sticking it out was even more of a challenge. Listen to the description by William Milne, the first assistant who joined him: "To acquire the Chinese [language] is a work for men with bodies of brass, lungs of steel, heads of oak, hands of spring steel, eyes of eagles, hearts of apostles, memories of angels, and lives of Methuselah."

Life is seldom a cakewalk for one who hears God call by desire. A calling is tenacious. It works itself out despite the obstacles. The Chinese Bible is testament to Robert Morrison's persistent pursuit of his calling against all odds.

✸ TAKING ACTION

1. Katharine Whitehorn said, *"The best careers advice to give to the young is 'Find out what you like doing best and get someone to pay you for doing it.'"* Do you agree? Disagree? Why?

   _____

   _____

   _____

2. What is something that compels, drives, and pushes you in life? It is something that can not be ignored or brushed aside. It is something that you cannot help but do.

   _____

   _____

   _____

3. If you were guaranteed a handsome salary regardless of which career you chose, what would you do?

   _____

   _____

   _____

4. How can God call us through "desire"?

   _____

   _____

5. What was the deep desire that drove Nehemiah? (See Nehemiah 1.)

_____

_____

6. Why is our contentment in our career or task so affected by our desire?

_____

_____

_____

7. Do you have a God-given calling that is rooted in desire? Evaluate your calling in light of the following statements and questions . . .

_____

_____

_____

- It *might* be calling by desire if . . . the sense of urgency is persistent and relatively long-standing. How long have you felt or known this calling by desire?

_____

_____

- It is probably *not* calling by desire if . . . I am completely unequipped to get the job done. Is your calling by desire something you feel equipped to accomplish?

_____

- It is probably *not* calling by desire if . . . I quit when I encounter significant hurdles. What price are you willing to pay to pursue this calling by desire?

_____

_____

CHAPTER 9

CALLED BY
ARRANGED PATH

"A MAN PLANS HIS STEPS, BUT GOD DIRECTS HIS PATH."

—SOLOMON

⚙ DRIVING THOUGHT

Sometimes calling is self-evident. It is not a question of what your calling is, but if you want to accept it.

⚙ DRILLING DOWN

King Edward VIII brought Great Britain to the edge of a constitutional crisis. He ascended to the English throne in January, 1936 as a bachelor, but during his first year of reign, he decided to marry Wallis Simpson, a newly divorced American woman he had met in 1930 while she was still married. Edward had no desire to leave the throne, but the Church of England would not accept their monarch marrying a divorcee.

Edward would have to choose between the woman he loved and the Crown. After a reign of just 325 days, Edward abdicated the throne on December 10, 1936, by signing the following two-sentence declaration:

I, Edward the Eighth, of Great Britain, Ireland, and the British Dominion beyond the Seas, King, Emperor of India, do hereby declare my irrevocable determination to renounce the Throne for myself and for my descendants, and my desire that effect should be given to this Instrument of Abdication immediately.

In token whereof I have hereunto set my hand this tenth day of December, nineteen hundred and thirty six, in the presence of the witnesses whose signatures are subscribed.

Edward R.I.
Signed at Fort Belvedere in the
presence of Albert Henry George

With those simple words, King Edward VIII walked away from his job. He later married Simpson and died in exile in Paris in 1972.

Edward's startling choice abruptly changed the British line of royal succession. His brother, Albert, became king. Albert's daughter, Elizabeth, would not be the queen of England today if it had not been for Edward's abdication. Elizabeth experienced how external events sometimes define the path of our calling. Yet each of us, like Edward, must decide whether to accept that mantle or walk away from it.

Sometimes calling is self-evident. It is not a question of what your calling is, but if you want to accept it. Edward was going to be king, unless he chose to walk away.

One of the ways God calls is to make things so certain that the individual affected might wrestle with *if* they want to do it, but not *what* they are supposed to do. Sometimes it is a golden opportunity that falls in your lap. Perhaps it is an extraordinary ability that you were born with. Other times it is an option that has God's fingerprints all over it.

Such gates of obvious calling usually are covered with risk, overwhelming fear, and intimidation on the front side, but almost always prove painted with unusual opportunity and gratification on the other.

MAKING EVALUATION

How can you discern if the path you are on is indeed arranged by God? How do you make sure you are not chasing a rabbit trail? Might it be an errand of your own making? As you prayerfully try to discern if you are called to a path arranged by God, here are several trail markers to look for:

IT *MIGHT* BE CALLING BY ARRANGED PATH IF . . . THE OBJECTIONS YOU FACE IN YOUR DECISION ARE NOT NEGATIVE CONSEQUENCES IF YOU DO IT, BUT IF YOU DON'T.

The calling of an obviously arranged path does not allow much space for choice, equivocation or ambiguity. It just seems clear cut—at least to most of those looking on. That doesn't mean that decisions do not have to be made. It just requires different kinds of choices. It is not a choice about *what* do to, but *whether* you want to do it. Its inherent inertia can be changed only by a choice to *not* do something. If, for example, you feel called to begin a new company and launch out as an entrepreneur, it is very possible—even probable—that the response you will hear from friends and family will move along the lines of:

- "Oh, really?"
- "You aren't honestly thinking of that, are you? Are you serious?"
- "Who else knows about this? What do they think?"
- "What if it doesn't work? Then what?"
- "What makes you think you will be good at this?"

Think, in contrast, what people must have thought about Edward not remaining king:

- "What is he thinking????"
- "How can he walk away from that kind of honor and privilege?"
- "He was born for this!!"
- "How dare he think he can just up and leave!?"

IT *MIGHT* BE CALLING BY ARRANGED PATH IF . . . WHAT EVERYONE ELSE EXPECTS MAKES LOGICAL SENSE TO ME, TOO.

Just because everyone else expects someone to fill a specific role is not enough by itself to qualify as God's call on their life. Calling is God's person-specific invitation. In the end, the individual being called must determine if the call is for him. You will stand before Jesus one day and give an account of your life, and it will not be good enough to say, "Everyone expected me to do it, and I never really thought much about it myself." Calling is something you answer to Jesus for; so whatever others think must be confirmed in your own spirit.

IT'S PROBABLY *NOT* CALLING BY ARRANGED PATH IF . . . THE TIMING IS OUT OF SYNC.

Prince Charles someday will be the King of England. When? Nobody knows. He is ready and has been for some time. He is getting older, already well into middle age. He has been called to that task since conception.

Charles will become the King of England when his mother decides it is time, or when she dies. He has very little to do with his highest calling. Until the crown is on his head, he is called to wait and to look as productive as possible. Charles must content himself that, at least for now, he is called to be a prince. It is not yet time for him to be king.

Because God has placed us in space and time, and "determined the times set for us and the exact places where we should live," (Acts 17:26 NIV) calling always operates within the boundaries of His timing. We are not called to do something at the wrong time. If the timing is out of sync, then the calling is incomplete.

✸ TAKING ACTION

1. What is a call "arranged by path"?

   _____

   _____

2. The key issue in call arranged by path is not what one is supposed to do, but _____.

3. Esther was an individual created and placed "for such a time as this." Describe the nature of her calling.

_____

_____

_____

4. Have you ever experienced an obvious call via your path or circumstance? Describe how you realized the call and responded.

_____

_____

_____

5. Do you know anyone who, like King Edward VIII, walked away from his "apparent calling" to pursue a "deeper calling"?

_____

_____

_____

6. How can you discern if the path you are on is indeed arranged by God? Might it be an errand of your own making? As you prayerfully try to discern if you are being called by a path arranged by God, here are several trail markers to use in evaluation. Read them and respond to the corresponding question:

   • It *might* be calling by arranged path if . . . the objections you face in your decision are not negative consequences if you do it, but if you don't.

Is your sense of calling arranged by path something you can't choose to ignore?

_____

_____

_____

- It *might* be calling by arranged path if . . . what everyone else expects makes logical sense to me, too.

  Is your sense of calling aligning with the expectations others have for you? Do any New Testament characters come to mind who were affirmed in their calling by others?

  _____

  _____

  _____

- It's probably *not* calling by arranged path if . . . the timing is out of sync.

  Is your sense of calling by arranged path confirmed by it being at the right time and at the right place? Are you in the zone on timing and direction?

  _____

  _____

  _____

CHAPTER 10

WHICH CALLING PLAN AM I ON?

"Calling is the Archemedian point by which faith moves the world."

—Os Guiness

⊛ Driving Thought

Calling is always crucial and often confusing. It requires constant attention through all the seasons of our lives.

⊛ Drilling Down

The Gdansk shipyard was an ordinary place to work. This Polish industrial complex that built huge oceangoing cargo vessels looked no different than one on the Houston shipping channel or in Norfolk or the port of Los Angeles. Every morning a herd of men with hard hats walked in carrying lunch boxes. After eight hours of welding, grinding, painting, operating cranes, driving forklifts and the like, the whistle sounded and a herd of hard hats headed home.

On August 14, 1980, the whistle blew, but nobody went home. Instead, one man jumped the fence and joined those already inside. His name was Lech Walesa, an electrician at the shipyard who had been fired for protesting the plight of workers in the face of staggering rises in food prices instituted by Poland's then Communist government. The whole shipyard came to a standstill as all the workers joined a sit-in strike demanding that Walesa be reinstated. Soon other factories joined in sympathy. Unrest among workers spread throughout Poland demanding reforms.

Facing the specter of a spreading insurrection and the very real threat of a Soviet threat to restore order, the Marxist president of Poland asked to negotiate with the workers. Walesa was chosen to represent them. As a result of these historic talks, the government allowed the organization of free trade unions. The next month, Walesa helped found Solidarity, the first free trade union in the communist world.

Solidarity thrived, spreading the dream of autonomy to every workplace in Poland, until December, when the boot descended once again. Martial law was declared. Walesa was arrested. By 1989, with social unrest once again rising, the communist party called for free elections, freed Walesa and asked for his help. Running under Solidarity, Walesa was overwhelmingly elected President of Poland.

How does an electrician go from a shipyard to the President's office? The answer is simple. He followed his calling, one step at a time. At first it was a vocation of choice, wiring ships. Then he was fired. Then it was the appealing opportunity to represent his coworkers negotiating for freedom. Then he was arrested. Eventually, by the time he was elected to lead a nation, it was clear that Walesa was an ordinary man following a path arranged by the Great Conductor of history.

Os Guiness is right. Calling is nothing less than an invitation by God to use our work to move the world. Exhilaration comes from knowing that your work assignment is from God and that you are uniquely designed by

Him to accomplish it. In the middle of the stress and sweat, the labor and tears, the ups and downs, the good and bad, the wins and losses should come some sense that "I am made to do this!"

The reality is that calling is often very difficult to pin down. A feeling of "career unsettledness" frequently invades our peace. Why does it have to be so hard? In theory, it should be rather straightforward. Jesus talks and, as His children, we listen. He has a task for us, and we are ready and eager to jump on it. He asks for our all, and we want to serve Him. All the same, many of us still don't know what to do. We are confused. Our desire to know is intense, precisely because we understand the stakes: Fulfillment. Meaning. Living a life of significance.

Calling is always crucial and often confusing. For some followers of Jesus calling comes with ease. For most believers, however, settling on their calling is a complex and mysterious process. It requires constant attention through all the seasons of their lives.

MAKING EVALUATION

There is no silver bullet in solving the calling question. The lack of an easy and immediate solution, however, does not mean that you cannot figure calling out. In fact, we know Jesus wants us to hear His voice. So how do you move forward? Consider this protocol of questions to work through in coming to conclusion and solution.

WHAT IS THE STATE OF MY RELATIONSHIP WITH JESUS?

Everything begins and ends with this: The vitality of our walk with

Christ. If we are not consistently in Scripture and on our knees in prayer, we will have little confidence that what we are thinking is what He is thinking. We have no right to take the calling matter into our own hands, and that is precisely what we do when we begin to make career decisions without being in a serious God-listening mode.

Wrestling with calling may benefit from fasting, and possibly some time off in a remote location to think, journal, and listen. Getting our heads in Scripture is also crucial. And it can be helpful to find and read significant devotional books. The bottom line: Hearing God's call involves putting ourselves in a position to hear God's voice.

WHAT SPECIFIC CLUES TELL ME THAT JESUS MAY BE STEERING ME TOWARD A CAREER OR JOB CHANGE?

A change of this magnitude does not happen out of thin air. What collection of indications have you experienced over what period of time that give you pause about what you are currently doing with your career? Has the Lord talked to you through Scripture? Is there a recurring thought that nags and will not go away? Do you feel a growing discontent with the current state of life? Are you drawn somewhere different? If so, why?

While identifying the signs of your potential calling, think through the three categories of how God actually calls listed in the previous chapters. Which does He seem to be using in your case? Journal as much of this pilgrimage as possible. Put it down in black and white and review it periodically. Submitting to that discipline helps you "size" the situation. What seems like a huge deal in the middle of the night may not feel the same way after it is written down and read in the light of day.

WHAT DO MY CIRCLE OF ADVISORS SAY?

We can't do life alone. We are built for community, and the strength of that fellowship comes into play during times of decision like this. A "circle of advisors" gives invaluable feedback. One might be your spouse, another your brother-in-law. Others may be lifelong peer friendships. And some may be mentors you trust to give godly advice.

When you go to them during this process, continue to supply up-to-date information that helps them give good advice. If you have been journaling, for example, share what you are thinking and why. Their value-add will not come in "giving the answer," but through probing questions, the telling of experiences of others who have walked this path, etc.

IS MY CURRENT CAREER MOVING ME TOWARD MY SKILL SET OR AWAY FROM IT?

It is possible that career unsettledness could come from an appropriate—though uncomfortable—set of challenges on the job. Scripture makes it clear that work life will not be easy, the sweat of labor will come with virtually any job we take anywhere.

In the process of listening to God's voice, distinguish between the actual job you have and the kind of work you do.

God often places us in challenging job situations as part of the work He is doing in us and as part of what He wants to do through us there. We need to be careful about assuming that He wants us to leave just because it is not much fun. Benjamin Franklin was right: "All human situations have their inconveniences. We feel those of the present but neither see nor feel those of the future; and hence we often make troublesome changes without amendment, and frequently for the worse."

Is the tension you feel the natural pain of God growing you in your work or a symptom of a bad fit? Sometimes it's time for a job change, and sometimes you are the one who needs to be changed.

✸ TAKING ACTION

1. Let's review. Name the three categories of how God calls us as listed in the previous chapters:

   a. _____

   b. _____

   c. _____

2. Has determining your calling been a difficult task? Why is discovering our calling so hard?

   _____

   _____

   _____

3. The intensity of the journey leading us to find our calling tells us that much is at stake. What is riding on our success or failure in determining our calling?

   _____

   _____

   _____

4. Circle the phrase that best describes your sense of calling:

   "I was made to do this."   *"Career unsettledness"*

5. What test can you take to determine your calling? There is no silver bullet in solving the calling question. The following questions can help establish some deeper thought and direction related to calling:

   • **What is the state of my relationship with Jesus?** We have no right to take the calling matter into our own hands, and that is precisely what we do when we begin to make career decisions without being in a serious God-listening mode.

   _____

   _____

   • **What specific clues tell me that Jesus may be steering me toward a career or job change?** A change of this magnitude does not happen out of thin air. What collection of indications have you experienced over what period of time that give you pause about what you are currently doing with your career?

   _____

   _____

   • **What do my circle of advisors say?** We are built for community and the strength of that fellowship comes into play during times of decision like this.

   _____

   _____

- **Is my current career moving me toward my skill set or away from it?**
  Is my current role preparing me and maturing me in my calling, even
  if the situation is not perfect?

  _____

  _____

SERVING@WORK

PEOPLE OF FAITH OUGHT TO *MODEL*
SERVING IN THEIR WORK.

Serving others. It doesn't come naturally. We are born bent in the opposite direction. Instead of a fine-tuned radar directed outward toward the needs of others, we usually are focused on taking care of number one. We are skilled at arranging information, opportunities, even relationships around our self-interested grid. "What's in it for me?" is often the single criteria.

Then, along came Jesus . . . the One who cast aside what was good for Himself and acted upon what was good for us. He broke the choke hold that self-centeredness has on us. It still might not come naturally, but as a person of faith we can learn the art of focusing on someone else's interest instead of our own.

Until we learn and embrace the discovery that it is not "all about me," we will never enjoy the deep fulfillment and pure goodness of helping others. When we are the constant center of the universe, our world of work always shrinks down to a boring, empty stillness.

SERVING

*is the art of focusing on someone
else's interest instead of my own.*

CHAPTER 11

SERVING NINE
TO FIVE

"It is not what a man does that determines whether his work is sacred or secular, but why he does it."

—A.W. Tozer

⊛ Driving Thought

Every job invites us to experience the five purposes of work: provision, character development, worship, modeling, and service to others.

⊛ Drilling Down

One night years ago when my oldest daughter was still a child, I was putting her to bed when she locked eyes with me and asked a question that almost every kid eventually poses to his/her dad or mom. "Daddy," she said, "Why do you have to get up every day and go to work? Why can't you just stay home and play all day with me?" Of course, I gave her the stock answer for a dad who doesn't have an answer: "Go ask your mom." No, actually I gave her my number two stock answer. I said, "Katelyn that is such a good question. Would you let me give you the answer tomorrow night?" True, it was way past her bedtime, but I was stalling.

That evening pushed my thinking. I sat on her bed as she slept, and I rehearsed every story from Scripture that I could think of that touched the world of work. The process that began that night reconfirmed my understanding of the divine reason I get up and go to work.

The next night, I tucked her in bed and was ready and loaded for bear. I had cued up my prepared fatherly presentation, ready to roll out the Theology of Work. I was equipped for questions and anything else that might come up. To my surprise and disappointment, however, she had forgotten the question. She wanted me to tell one of my nightly stories of Bandit, the mysterious black squirrel.

She might have been distracted with Bandit for the moment, but she will have to answer these questions herself one day: What motivations can pull us out of bed even on dreary rainy mornings? Knowing that the day holds explosive pressure and demands, what pushes us through the dark door of work for one more day? In short, why work?

MAKING EVALUATION

As we discussed in Chapter 2, a solid theology of work sees work as something good, as something God ordained before the Fall and as something that will take toil and sweat to accomplish after the Fall. Work, however, has several significant God-ordained purposes. There are at least five: Provision, character development, worship, modeling, and service to others.

PROVISION

On the most primary level, work provides the necessities of physical life: food, drink, clothing, and shelter. Work is a God-given vehicle for meeting our needs. Any individual capable of work should do it. Whether paid or voluntary, at home or in the Oval Office, work is not an option.

The Bible, especially in the wisdom literature and Pauline theology, is pregnant with warnings against idleness and exhortations to live productively. Paul is blunt and to the point: "If a man will not work, he shall not eat" (2 Thess. 3:10; see also vv. 11, 12 NIV). There is no biblical support for the dreamy days of retirement. Regular work should be a part of our routine until the day we die. It might slow down or be redefined, but without work, rest will never totally make sense.

CHARACTER DEVELOPMENT

Life is classroom. It's a place for growth. We don't always succeed, but even our failures—and maybe *especially* our failures—contributed to the development of our character.

In the crucible of the business world with its amoral worship of "whatever works," we have to remove the moral sludge from our lives and understand in vivid terms the meaning of Peter's admonishment:

Make every effort to add to your faith goodness; and to goodness, knowledge; and to knowledge, self-control; and to self-control, perseverance; and to perseverance, godliness; and to godliness, brotherly kindness; and to brotherly kindness, love. For if you possess these qualities in increasing measure, they will keep you from being ineffective and unproductive in your knowledge of our Lord Jesus Christ (2 Pet. 1:5–8 NIV).

WORSHIP

Work and worship at first sound like an oxymoron. We work at the office, and we worship at church. A quick tour of Scripture, though, provides a surprising list of the places where we are called to worship God: on the mountain, in the desert, in Hebron, at His sanctuary, on the Mount of Olives, in bed, in the temple, on the battlefields, in the heavens, in front of gates, in Jerusalem, in Judah, in Babylon, in a manger in Bethlehem, at feasts, and at the feet of angels. In short, we should worship God wherever God happens to be. Of course, that means everywhere.

It's not so much where we are or what we're doing as it is for whom we are doing it. Charles Swindoll hit the nail on the head, as usual, when he remarked, "We have become a generation of people who worship our work, who work at our play, and who play at our worship." Honoring God through what we do is not something that comes naturally. We must work at worshiping God in all arenas: the office, our playground, and our sanctuary.

MODELING

If our lives are a living sacrifice, then we can initiate an act of worship for others. They look at our lives, our God-given skills, our blessings, our sense of joy and peace, and they ascribe value to God. We reflect Him, causing others to worship Him. As Edith Wharton noted, "There are two ways of spreading light: to be the candle or the mirror that reflects it." God is our only source of light, but we must be a mirror so that others can see Him, too.

We do that by staying connected to Jesus. "I am the vine; you are the branches," Jesus said in John 15:5. "If a man remains in me and I in him, he will bear much fruit; apart from me you can do nothing" (NIV). Growing the Life@Work we were designed for means tapping into the Vine. It means staying connected to God, the only sustaining life source. As we abide in

Him, the fruit He will grow in our lives will include the Life@Work quartet of evidencing His calling; displaying character; delivering skill; and serving others.

Only as we learn of the life and character of Jesus can we begin to reflect His words and deeds in our own Life@Work. Slowly, He re-creates us into the people we were originally created to be: fully human, uniquely gifted, natural in worship, and tirelessly productive. Our work begins to work as a light does in a dark place.

SERVICE TO OTHERS

The work God intends for us always involves a mindset of service to others. Our model is Christ, who in giving up the prerogatives of being God to take on human flesh exemplified for us meekness, commitment, servanthood, humility, and obedience.

Work is designed as both grand and mysterious. We have the opportunity, through simple acts motivated by a spirit of service to participate with God in the day-to-day spinning of His world. In this sense, the plumber, the preacher, the policeman, and the pool keeper all stand on level ground. Whether unclogging drains or souls or streets or filters, each person contributes a necessary good to the world.

This utilitarian component of work has nothing to do with "me and my needs." We are supposed to be part of that big "work" machine in life. Our work somehow makes the world a better place. At the end of the day, if it is all about "me and my money," then we have left out something of primary importance: Service to humanity. With ability comes reciprocal responsibility. As Barbara Sher has noted, "Being gifted creates obligations, which means you owe the world your best effort at the work you love. You, too, are a natural resource." How much even more so from a faith view of life!

✸ TAKING ACTION

1. Circle the phrase that best represents the majority of your thinking toward work:

   "Work is a curse."   *"Work is a potential blessing."*

   Why have you felt this way?

   _____

   _____

   _____

2. Would work exist if Adam had not sinned? Why do you say so?

   _____

   _____

   _____

3. Work has five God-ordained purposes. Write a brief explanation of how each of these is accomplished through your work:

   Provision

   _____

   _____

Character Development

_____

_____

Worship

_____

_____

Modeling

_____

_____

Service to others

_____

_____

4. Which of the purposes of work come most naturally to you and which are more of a challenge?

_____

_____

_____

_____

5. Look through the following verses and sort them against the five purposes of work: Proverbs 6:6–11; 10:4, 5; 10:26; 12:24; 12:27; 13:4; 14:23; 15:19; 18:9; 19:15; 19:24; 20:4; 20:13; 21:25, 26; 24:30–34;

26:14–16; Ecclesiastes 4:5; 10:18; Isaiah 56:10; 1 Timothy 5:13, 14; 1 Timothy 5:8; 2 Peter 1:5–8; Colossians 3:23; Psalm 63; John 15:5; Philippians 2:3–5; Acts 11:29; 2 Corinthians 8:4.

_____

_____

_____

_____

_____

_____

_____

_____

CHAPTER 12

IT'S NOT
ABOUT ME

"I DON'T KNOW WHAT YOUR DESTINY WILL BE, BUT ONE THING I DO KNOW: THE ONLY ONES AMONG YOU WHO WILL BE REALLY HAPPY ARE THOSE WHO HAVE SOUGHT AND FOUND HOW TO SERVE."

—ALBERT SCHWEITZER

❋ Driving Thought

Serving has to be the core of our Life@Work or it won't have a core at all.

❋ Drilling Down

Alfred Nobel invented dynamite. He is most famous, however, for what he did with the fortune he made from it. He established a trust to create a prize recognizing individuals who have marked our globe with exceptional service toward humankind. Since 1901 the Nobel Foundation in Stockholm, Sweden, has awarded Nobel prizes to such recipients as Albert Schweitzer, Martin Luther King, Jr., and Bishop Desmond Tutu. None set out to win the Nobel Prize or to receive its worldwide fame and huge cash award. Their motivation was simply to help and serve others. The 1921 Nobel Prize winner for physics, Albert Einstein, said it best: "Only a life lived in the service to others is worth living."

Few Nobel Prize winners have captured the heart of the world more than the small, frail nun from Albania. Mother Teresa won the Nobel Peace Prize in 1979 for her work among the destitute, the dying, and the orphan children in the slums of Calcutta, India.

As an inscription on her tombstone, Mother Teresa requested these words of Jesus from the Gospel of John: "Love me as I have loved you." As Saint Augustine wrote: "There is something in humility which strangely exalts the heart." Mother Teresa was a humble servant if ever there was one, and we are all better for her life's work.

What will be said of us when we die? Will anyone be better off because of our life's work? What will they carve on our tombstones? What ten-word inscription on a rock will sum up our lives?

If one of those words doesn't convey "service," then our life will have been a tragic waste of self-indulgence. Contrary to conventional wisdom, the bottom line of a career is not how far we advance ourselves, but how far we advanced and served others.

Service is a central component of the message of Christianity. There are more than a thousand references to servant, serving, and service in the sixty-six books of the Bible. It is a quality that God emphasizes and elevates as a universal language for all who have passed beneath the Cross of Christ.

But what is serving at its core? When stripped to the basics, what does it mean and what does it look like? And how do we live this definition of serving: *Serving is the art and act of focusing on someone else's interest, not my own.*

That definition demands a role reversal for most of us in this culture where self-driven, self-deserved attention is the common currency.

To start our journey toward a lifetime of service, each of us must redraw the universe around others, not ourselves. As John the Baptist said to Jesus, "You must increase and I must decrease."

Joe White, founder of the nationally known Kanukkuk Camps in Branson, Missouri, calls this the "I am third" philosophy. God is first, others are second, and I am always third. At Kanukkuk, the highest recognition passed out each week of camp is the "I am third Award." Most offices today are dominated by the competition for the "I am first award." How much different would they look if they were defined instead by an "I am third" philosophy?

What would our work lives look like if they were restructured upon such a foundation. One thing is for sure: Our places of work would not be the same.

MAKING EVALUATION

Jesus was a servant. We should be servants.

It sounds easy enough. But what does an attitude of service look like to each of us in our personal, individualized worlds?

The apostle Paul paints a scene that draws out the implications of Jesus' example as a servant for us. In it, Paul is explaining the distinguishing characteristics of his Master to a new group of believers, the Phillipians:

> "If you've gotten anything at all out of following Christ, if his love has made any difference in your life, if being in a community of the Spirit means anything to you, if you have a heart, if you care—then do me a favor: Agree with each other, love each other, be deep-spirited friends. Don't push your way to the front; don't sweet-talk your way to the top. Put yourself

aside, and help others get ahead. Don't be obsessed with getting your own advantage. Forget yourselves long enough to lend a helping hand.

Think of yourselves the way Christ Jesus thought of himself. He had equal status with God but didn't think so much of himself that he had to cling to the advantages of that status no matter what. Not at all. When the time came, he set aside the privileges of deity and took on the status of a slave, became human! Having become human, he stayed human. It was an incredibly humbling process. He didn't claim special privileges. Instead, he lived a selfless, obedient life and then died a selfless, obedient death—and the worst kind of death at that: a crucifixion" (Phil. 2:1–11 MSG).

No example of selflessness will ever be greater than what Jesus Christ did. Some of the most clearheaded insights on serving to ever be found are found in this passage. Consider these questions, based on the passage, to see how well you understand the concepts of Christ-centered service.

DO YOU CLUTCH TOO TIGHTLY THE THINGS THAT "RIGHTFULLY" BELONG TO YOU? (V. 6)

Sound theology says things don't really belong to us—they are on loan from God, and we are only stewards. Practically speaking, however, we feel as if things do belong to us, and so we clutch those things tightly. We hold and we hoard. We hide and we stash. We maneuver and manipulate. To unravel this death grip of selfishness, we have to pry our fingers off what we are holding onto. Giving them up means holding them with an open hand. We have to voluntarily give up our rights and prerogatives. There is no other path to servanthood.

DO YOU TAKE ON THE "PERSPECTIVE" OF THE ONE YOU ARE TRYING TO SERVE? (VV. 7, 8)

Jesus practiced the ultimate "walk in the other person's shoes for a day." The Incarnation was Him taking on the cloak of humanity. There is no part of my world or yours that Jesus does not know and understand. He knew us before we were born, and He knows us by experience. The big news, however, is that He feels every step of our pain and confusion. "Because he himself suffered when he was tempted, he is able to help those who are being tempted" (Heb. 2:18 NIV). Jesus can relate. He has been there. He chose to go there for you and me. Serving requires walking in the shoes of those you are trying to help.

WILL YOU SERVE EVEN WHEN YOUR ACTS OF SERVING GO UNNOTICED, MISUNDERSTOOD, OR EVEN REJECTED? (V. 8)

It happened with Jesus, and it will happen with us. We will go the second mile to help, and no one will say thanks. As a matter of fact, many times no one even sees us go the first mile, much less the second. Serving others means we must be satisfied to live with rewards that only God hands out. It is not a public award ceremony but a private prize within our own minds and hearts. We must take the approach of Seneca: "Be silent as to services you have rendered, but speak of favors you have received."

DO YOU RECOGNIZE THAT THE NEXT WORLD, NOT THIS ONE, IS WHERE THE SERVING GETS REWARDED? (VV. 9–11)

One thing bonds all those who serve together. They are moved toward a longer view of goodness. It is the pull of the next world that provides the strength and perspective to take on the good of another. As one bumper sticker says, "Come work for the Lord. The work is hard, the hours are long, and the pay is low, but the retirement benefits are out of this world."

✺ TAKING ACTION

1. Define serving. What is serving at its core?

   _____

   _____

   _____

2. What re-ordering of priorities is required to truly serve?

   _____

   _____

   _____

3. Consider these questions, based on Philippians 2:1–11, to see how well you understand the concepts of Christ-centered service.

- **Do you clutch too tightly the things that "rightfully" belong to you?** (v. 6) Sound theology says things don't really belong to us—they are on loan from God, and we are only stewards.

List 5 things you frequently clutch too tightly.

1. _____
2. _____
3. _____
4. _____
5. _____

How can you better comprehend the concept of stewardship versus ownership?

_____

_____

_____

_____

- **Do you take on the "perspective" of the one you are trying to serve?** (vv. 7, 8) Serving requires walking in the shoes of those you are trying to help. Put yourself in your boss's shoes a couple of days. Allow that adjusted perspective to "improve your serve."

_____

_____

_____

- **Will you serve even when your acts of serving go unnoticed, misunderstood, or even rejected?** (v. 8) Serving others means we must be satisfied to live with rewards that only God hands out. Name a time when you observed sacrificial serving that to your knowledge went unnoticed by others.

  _____

  _____

  _____

  _____

- **Do you recognize that the next world, not this one, is where serving gets rewarded?** (vv. 9–11) It is the pull of the next world that provides the strength and perspective to take on the good of another. Name three emotions that this statement evokes.

  1. _____

  2. _____

  3. _____

4. How can you incorporate serving others into your regular Life@Work?

  _____

  _____

  _____

5. Can you remember a situation in which you where on the receiving end of servanthood? How did it make you feel to be served?

_____

_____

_____

_____

_____

_____

_____

_____

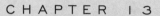

CHAPTER 13

EVERYDAY SAMARITAN

"THERE IS THE GREAT MAN WHO MAKES EVERY MAN FEEL SMALL, BUT THE REALLY GREAT MAN IS THE MAN WHO MAKES EVERY MAN FEEL GREAT."

—G.K. CHESTERTON

✵ DRIVING THOUGHT

To serve others every day in our Life@Work, we have to see like a
Samaritan, feel like a Samaritan, and act like a Samaritan.

✵ DRILLING DOWN

Have you ever been stranded?

Have you ever spent the night in an airport, trapped by weather delays
or, worse, an airline that overbooked the flight? Have you ever found yourself on the side of the highway, your car engine smoking and no town within
twenty miles in any direction? Worse, still, have you ever been mugged?
Beaten up, bruised and robbed? Or have you ever been so down-and-out
that you had no one to turn to and no place to go?

Jesus told a parable of a stranded traveler in need of help. Captured by
the Gospel writer Luke, the story's well-known as "The Good Samaritan." It
is the story of a traveler who was pounding the dust from one first-century

town to the next, a commonplace everyday routine from the days of the New Testament. The parable gives a terrific snapshot of serving in action.

This particular path was the only connector between Jerusalem and Jericho. Its seventeen miles of twisting and turning dirt road through high desert had a reputation for its bandits. People usually traveled in groups to ensure protection from the robbers and gangs. Sometimes, however, they simply had to risk the trip and go alone.

Such was the unfortunate case for the fellow in the story Jesus told. While making his way on the road through the pass, he was attacked, robbed, and left for dead. Eventually, along came the rest of the cast, three would-be helpers. Any of the three could have stopped, but only one took the time and effort to offer aid.

Ironically, the two who kept right on going were highly religious Jewish clerics. Even more paradoxically, the one who went out of his way to give first aid was a Samaritan, a group whom Jesus' Jewish audience would have least expected to help. Jews had deep enmity for Samaritans, despising them as "half-breeds" and religious heretics.

Jesus' use of irony always has a purpose. Faith is not about self-ascribed identity or mere declared belief, but about action, about serving our neighbors whoever they may be.

The central message Jesus hoped to drive deep with this parable is found with the answer to a single, simple question: "Who is my 'neighbor'?"

Jesus was challenging His audience with the way they treated all people. He wanted His followers to realize that the scope of serving others was much broader than their two or three best friends. Every day we, too, are faced with the question, "Who is my neighbor?" We see people needing help. A family about to be bumped from a flight. A colleague scrambling to meet a client's eleventh hour demand. An office mate whose car will not start. A competitor in the convention booth next to us who gets sick at a trade show. A client who asks for help on something we don't get a commission on.

Who exactly qualifies as our neighbor? The implicit question is, "Do I have to help *them?*" The answer was unmistakable in the first-century story, and it is undeniable today. Our neighbor is anyone who comes across our path who needs help that we can provide. Jesus calls us to be an Everyday Samaritan.

MAKING EVALUATION

There are three elements to serving other people as an Everyday Samaritan: Seeing like a Samaritan. Feeling like a Samaritan. Acting like a Samaritan.

SEEING LIKE AN EVERYDAY SAMARITAN

In this story all three could-be angels of assistance were confronted with the broken, beaten up man laying over in the rocks, but they did not all *see* the same thing. The first two were religious hypocrites who only saw a ceremonially unclean carcass; if they touched it, they would become ceremonially unclean, as well. They had a blind spot to need that was created by their own self-styled religion. The Samaritan saw a fellow human being in trouble; he saw an opportunity to serve.

We, too, can have blind spots. It is easy to have eyes and yet not see. The power of observation is something that must be learned. Dr. William Osler, a celebrated medical professor of the early 1900's, became famous for taking classes full of young medical students and having them spend days, not just hours, studying and documenting in their journals as many observations about a single microscope slide specimen as they possibly could. His conviction was that a physician who had honed his observation skills would be a better doctor.

People all around us are hurting and needy. Do we see . . .

1. People who are stripped of self-confidence, self-worth, hope, faith, purity, meaning, and opportunity?

2. People who are beaten by competition, by failure, by pressure to perform?

3. People who are abandoned, lonely, gripped by fear and doubt?

Stop today and look around the office. Are you seeing what is really there? Do you see the single mom with bloodshot eyes from long hours struggling to make it for her kids? Do you see the manager down the hall whose marriage is on the rocks? When you see your boss you despise, do you see the rebellious teenager at his home? That employee who frustrates you— do you notice the burden she carries of raising a special needs child?

The ability to spot people around us who are in need of serving is the first step toward practicing everyday serving. Three different men traveled by the beat-up traveler. They all saw him lying there . . . but what did each really see?

FEELING LIKE AN EVERYDAY SAMARITAN

Three guys walked along the same path and encountered the same scene. A priest, then a Levite, then a detested Samaritan. Two could not walk by fast enough. One stood out because he stopped to give aid. Why did he stop?

Jesus doesn't leave it to our imagination. Jesus said it was deep sympathy that drove the heart of the Samaritan to help. One translation calls it pity or compassion. He was moved deep in his heart with empathy—an emotion that is shared *with* someone. Here the key word is *with*—making the link between one person and the other person. Empathy requires us to connect with the interior of our own life, not just a surface, shallow frown of sympathy.

Someone once observed, "The greatest feats of love are performed by those who have had much practice in performing daily acts of kindness." It takes empathy to do that. And empathy grows with use. As the bumper sticker says, "Practice random acts of kindness and senseless beauty."

ACTING LIKE AN EVERYDAY SAMARITAN

We already know that only one traveler stopped and provided help. The Samaritan saw the man in need; he empathetically felt his pain and stopped to help the injured man. What did it take for the Samaritan to put feet to his feelings? More to the point, how can we practically serve others as we go through our workdays?

IT TAKES INITIATIVE. The Samaritan took a relational chance. He knew he was probably hated and disliked by the Jewish victim in the road, but he took the risk anyway. He stopped and reached out his hand not knowing what the response might be.

IT TAKES ADJUSTMENT. The Samaritan obviously was going somewhere. It's unlikely that his calendar called for roaming around Jericho looking for assault victims to help. He obviously missed his appointment and had his schedule wrecked that day. Effective serving sometimes means accepting inconvenience.

IT TAKES SACRIFICE. The Samaritan gave his time, his money, and his compassion. He obviously got his hands dirty helping clean up the stripped, beaten man. The story as told by Jesus even says that he instructed the innkeeper to keep a tab of the cost to convalesce the assaulted man and he would take care of the entire debt.

✸ TAKING ACTION

1. What can we learn about serving from the story of the Good Samaritan found in Luke 10:29–37?

   _____

   _____

   _____

2. What does it mean to "*see* like an everyday Samaritan"?

   _____

   _____

   _____

3. Close your eyes and *look* around your office. Who do you see in need? Your neighborhood?

   _____

   _____

4. What does it mean to "*feel* like an everyday Samaritan"?

   _____

_____

_____

5. Can you remember a time in your life in which you were in great need of help? How can this situation help you in understanding the needs of others?

_____

_____

_____

6. What does it mean to "*act* like an everyday Samaritan"?

_____

_____

_____

7. Acting like an Everyday Samaritan requires initiative, adjustment, and sacrifice. Think of someone in your everyday context that could use a "Good Samaritan," then fill in the following action plan for service:

Name _____

How can you take initiative to serve?

_____

_____

What adjustments in your routine will you have to make?

_____

_____

What sacrifice will your service require?

_____

_____

8. What are some things that hinder you from being an "Everyday Samaritan?

_____

_____

_____

9. Grade your everyday Samaritan traits 1–10.
   • "Seeing like an everyday Samaritan" _____
   • "Feeling like an everyday Samaritan" _____
   • "Acting like an everyday Samaritan" _____

CHAPTER 14

THE DIFFERENT FACES OF SERVING

"A Christian man is a perfectly free lord of all, subject to none. A Christian man is a perfectly dutiful servant, subject to all."

—Martin Luther

⊛ DRIVING THOUGHT

Serving others in our Life@Work extends in at least four directions: up, out, down, and across.

⊛ DRILLING DOWN

It was a beautiful fall Saturday morning in Arkansas. Red, yellow, and orange leaves speckled the backyard out our breakfast room window. A change of seasons was in the air. My daughter and I sat across the kitchen table looking through a stack of brochures as we ate Krispy Kreme Doughnuts©. The seasons were changing in our family, as well. She was a senior in high school, and it was time to pick a college.

"What do you think about Samford, Dad?" she said, handing me a glossy recruiting booklet. I could tell she was watching my eyes for a reaction. It was not a random question. Her mom graduated from Samford, and a number of kids we knew had gone there. As we leafed through the pages of the brochure, one thing became obvious: Samford was laying out its best pitch to potential customers. It reminded me of a quip from Mark Twain: "Many a small thing has been made large by the right kind of advertising" (*A Connecticut Yankee in King Arthur's Court*).

The admissions brochure highlighted all of the key factors any parent and child would look for in a school. In other words, it put forth the best "faces" of the university. There was one whole section showing the face of "fun for the student." It showed photo after photo of collegians laughing and enjoying life at sports events, socials, and even the Birmingham nightlife. My daughter's first response was the intended outcome: "Dad, this place looks fun."

Another objective obviously was to allay safety concerns of parents. There was a two-page spread of the entire campus displaying a tight, boundaried community. Sprinkled throughout were confidence-building snapshots of a mature, stable, and experienced faculty, all geared toward posturing the school's "safety face."

It also sought to present Samford as a "quality education for the money." The back of the brochure had an extensive list of available majors and minors—more than enough to overwhelm the future freshman. My daughter laughed and said, "What don't they offer at Samford?"

Whoever designed the brochure clearly understood that every college opportunity has a number of customers with different questions that must be satisfied in order to make the sale complete. Therefore, they strike their different poses and frame their different faces. Such comprehensive market analysis and pitch is the bread and butter of American business. Serving also has a number of customers. When it comes to serving, unfortunately, we are not as adroit at identifying all of the potential end-users.

If we analyzed our potential for serving at work, we would find that serving extends in at least four possible directions.

Serving Up—to our boss and superiors.

Serving Out—to our clients, customers, and patients.

Serving Down—to our employees, staff, and subordinates.

Serving Across—to our peers and competitors.

There are people on all sides of us. Often, however, we see them as a crowd and not as individuals. Folk-singer icon Joan Baez shared of herself, "The easiest kind of relationship for me is with ten thousand people. The hardest is with one." The bright lights of business can be just as blinding as stardom. In the end, work is always a people business. It is all about people with needs; yet many individuals we work around every day remain under our radar.

Making Evaluation

One way to evaluate where we are and where we need to go is to examine the lives of those who've led the way. Spend some time evaluating your service to others in these four categories in light of these examples:

Serving Up—to our boss and superiors

Ted Melvin is a 48-year-old executive with a Fortune 100 company and a history of serving his boss through extraordinary competence.

Ted tries to carry out his duties in the same way Joseph served Potiphar thousands of years ago. According to the Old Testament, all Potiphar had to worry about was what he would eat and what he would drink. Everything else he put in Joseph's charge.

This model of serving, however, requires something from Ted. It means he must work for extraordinary competence. Ted has to practice a "Promises Made—Promises Kept" mentality. He focuses to deliver results every day in his job. He works to keep his skills sharp. It takes a bedrock marriage of sound character with admirable ability. The result is that when Ted is done with his workday, the only thing left for his boss to figure out is the menu.

SERVING OUT—TO OUR CLIENTS, CUSTOMERS, AND PATIENTS

Cliff Ivers never liked going to the dentist, which is one of the reasons he operates his dental practice by adhering to a modified version of the Golden Rule: Treat your patients the way you would want to be treated if you were the one in the chair.

This isn't assembly-line dentistry with a "drill 'em, fill 'em, and bill 'em" mentality. He's committed to something more personal, and it extends to every aspect of his office. Cliff tries to view his entire work world through the patient's eyes. What do they see when they come through the door? How does everything from the wallpaper to the waiting room, to the magazines affect the patient's mood?

Cliff makes a deliberate attempt to create an office style that is friendly to his patients. That means he has to be upbeat and encouraging. He insists that his employees wear a warm smile regardless of the weather outside or office problems inside.

All of these things are important parts of Cliff's goal of serving his patients. Cliff realized that when you come down to it, his business is not just about delivering good teeth but serving up smiles.

SERVING DOWN—TO OUR EMPLOYEES, STAFF, AND SUBORDINATES

Jim Allen's vocation is all about serving others, but this minister of a growing church realizes there is a tendency to overlook the people who are paid to serve him. It is a common pitfall for busy bosses. They are eager to serve their clients, customers, or, in this case, parishioners, but in doing so, they ignore the needs of their hardworking staff.

Jim tries to avoid this pitfall by practicing what he calls "water-fountain management." He visits the water fountain with a purpose, intentionally spending time with staff members he meets there or along the way, learning their worlds, their hopes and their dreams, their problems and their victories.

If he knows their needs, he is more likely to meet them. That is why he offered a hand to the building superintendent when it came time to lift a new partition for an addition to the church office. Jim didn't have to find out about the man's back problem by hearing a scream of agony from a wrenched muscle. He already knew about it because he had talked to him and listened.

SERVING ACROSS—TO OUR PEERS AND COMPETITORS

Kimberly Thomas built her career in sales and marketing on a hard-charging zeal for being the best, but she sometimes alienated her peers and intimidated her coworkers.

Tired of feeling walls with those around her, she eventually realized she was not inspirational to those around her. She motivated with goals, not encouragement. She always talked numbers, not dreams.

It wasn't easy, but Kim retooled. She found that inspiration is always welcome and in much demand. Inspiration never intimidates and it certainly does not alienate. Inspiration causes people to believe in themselves. Through an inspirational encounter, even her competitors determined to become better and do their best.

Now Kim helps other people win. She doesn't play games. She is always honest. She is transparent. She is as much about the heart as she is the head or hands. She makes people feel better about themselves and better about the work they are called to do. Robert Louis Stevenson said, "Keep your fears to yourself, but share your inspiration with others" (xxiii, *Inspire* book).

There is something powerful about inspiration. It is a leveraged investment in people. For its minimal cost, it yields high returns. In the long run, growing the people around you through inspiration can only grow your agenda as well.

⊛ TAKING ACTION

1. List the four types of people we can Serve@Work as mentioned in the chapter:

   a. _____

   b. _____

   c. _____

   d. _____

2. What is meant by *serving up*?

   _____

_____

_____

3. Read Genesis 39:1–6. How did Joseph *serve up* to Potiphar?

_____

_____

_____

4. Name three ways you specifically *serve up* in your context?

   a. _____

   b. _____

   c. _____

5. What is meant by *serving out?*

_____

_____

_____

6. Give an example of an organization or a person who has modeled *serving out*:

_____

_____

_____

7. Name three ways you specifically *serve out* in your context?

   a. _____

b. _____

c. _____

8. What is meant by *serving down*?

_____

_____

_____

9. How did Jesus model *serving down*?

_____

_____

_____

10. Name three ways you specifically *serve down* in your context?

a. _____

b. _____

c. _____

11. What is meant by *serving across*?

_____

_____

12. How can serving across benefit both you and your coworkers?

_____

_____

13. Name three ways you specifically *serve across* in your context?

   a. _____

   b. _____

   c. _____

CHARACTER@WORK

PEOPLE OF FAITH OUGHT TO *DISPLAY CHARACTER* IN THE THEIR WORK.

Character matters.

Personality helps. Drive and focus make a difference. Passion plays a part. Education contributes. Connections open doors. But don't dare go to work without character.

Don't let anybody tell you otherwise. Character counts. You can take it to the bank. If you ignore it in yourself or others, you do so at your peril. It is a simple fact of business. Call it wisdom. Call it common sense. Or call it the gospel. Character is a bottom line issue. Period.

Don't hire anyone who doesn't have proven character. Don't accept a job from a boss without character. Don't even think about partnering with anyone in business who doesn't have it. Beware of customers or suppliers who are known to lack it. Be wary of colleagues who compromise it. Always keep your eye on the character quotient. Why?

Because character matters.

CHARACTER

is the sum of my behaviors, public and private,
consistently arranged across the spectrum of my life.

CHAPTER 15

THE ART OF ETCHING CHARACTER

"THE FINEST WORKERS IN STONE ARE NOT COPPER OR STEEL TOOLS, BUT THE GENTLE TOUCHES OF AIR AND WATER WORKING AT THEIR LEISURE WITH A LIBERAL ALLOWANCE OF TIME."

—HENRY DAVID THOREAU

❊ DRIVING THOUGHT

The lines of our behavior draw a picture of our character.

❊ DRILLING DOWN

My son and I were standing in the middle of the U.S. Capitol Rotunda, staring straight up one-hundred-and-eighty feet into the eye of the dome. The air was thick with history and a sense of the past.

It had only been a few weeks since the death of President Ronald Reagan, and his body had lain in state in this very room for mourners to visit. Flags were still at half-staff. As our tour group began to move on, I felt the need to pause in the middle of the rotunda. Why? The same reason the whole country had stopped for a week of grief and reflection. We had lost a rare leader, a man of character.

Standing there, I thought of Peggy Noonan's book on Reagan. The title says it all: *When Character Was King.*

I looked up at the ceiling of the Rotunda. The inner side of the dome is a fresco called "The Apotheosis of Washington." It is a scene of George Washington's ascent to heaven. It portrays Washington as the model ruler governing out of uncorrupted character. The theme of character continues around the outside walls of the Rotunda. Encircling us as we stood in the center of the room were statues of some of our most esteemed Americans—Abraham Lincoln, Martin Luther King, Jr., and Susan B. Anthony, among others.

The scene reminded me of a comment by General H. Norman Schwarzkopf—"Leadership is a potent combination of strategy and character. But if you must be without one, be without the strategy."

The word for "character" in the Bible comes from the Greek term describing an engraving instrument. The picture is of an artist who wears a groove on a metal plate by repeatedly etching the same place with a sharp tool. After repeated strokes an image begins to take shape.

Our character is forged as a set of distinctive marks that when taken together draw a portrait of who we really are. Everyone has character and it can be described: bad or good, shifty or sturdy, sordid or sterling.

Behavior and character are related, but they are not the same. Behavior is what we do. Character is the person our behavior has made us into. Behavior is just one action. Any behavior, duplicated and reduplicated, forms a part of our character.

Sometimes our portrait is compelling and attractive. In other cases it is ugly and repelling. Usually it is a combination of the two. Even great faces have warts.

Everything we do, every thought, every choice is a wave with ripple effects. It is easier to see their immediate effect on others than it is to see their consequence on the rock core of our own character. Yet if we look at the contours of our lives, we will clearly see the grooves shaped by the pattern of our past. As Anthony Robbins put it, "It is in your moments of decision that your destiny is shaped."

MAKING EVALUATION

The Old Testament's King David was a man of great courage, great loyalty, and great compassion, but he also fell to the temptations of his flesh. His life offers many valuable lessons on creating and managing our character. Let's take a look at a few and see how they might apply to our lives.

LESSON ONE: TAKE OWNERSHIP OF YOUR CHARACTER

Governing our character is very different from knowing our gift mix or our internal wiring. We are gifted and wired by God to be able to do certain things incredibly well. But no matter how hard we work at improving our abilities in other areas, we may never do them as well as someone who is gifted and wired in different ways.

We do have control, however, over our character. We can improve it, change it, modify it, or compromise it. In a world where we seem to have little control, we call the shots when it comes to whether or not our character is diminished. It was true for David, and it's true for you and me. Job said to his friends concerning his character: "I will not deny my integrity. I will maintain my righteousness and never let go of it; my conscience will not reproach me as long as I live" (Job 27:5, 6 NIV).

Do you take full ownership of your character?

Lesson Two: Start your pattern early and don't let up

An ancient Chinese proverb says, "Sow a thought, reap an act. Sow an act, reap a habit. Sow a habit, reap a character. Sow a character, reap a destiny." It's a truth the Bible seconds: "Do not be deceived. God is not mocked. Whatever a man sows, this he will also reap" (Gal. 6:7 NASB).

David became a giant-slayer long before he faced a giant. When he got flock-duty and his older brothers didn't, he obeyed his father even though it did not seem fair. Sitting in the field with the sheep all night, he chose to worship God to ward off his loneliness and fear. When a lion and a bear attacked the flock, he protected them.

As an adult, David was a man of humility, loyalty, courage, responsibility, and a soft tender heart. A timeline of his life would root those character traits right back to his early years.

How have your early years shaped your character?

Lesson Three: Over-manage your Achilles

David had many fine qualities, but as Oswald Sanders observed, "David's sensitive and artistic nature laid him open to temptation that would have bypassed one of a different texture" (Sanders, p. 121).

We all struggle with one or two sins of the heart that are unique to our make up. Although we are all vulnerable to every kind of sin, there is almost always at least one sin of the heart that persistently stalks us. It is crucial to our character that we know what it is and how to protect ourselves.

What temptation or temptations make up your Achilles heel? Identify it. Manage it. Build boundaries to protect yourself from your own weakness.

LESSON FOUR: CHARACTER IS NOT ABOUT PERFECTION

None of us is perfect, and David was no exception. He had a wild, misguided stroke on his character canvas: He committed adultery with Bathsheeba and killed her husband to cover it up. Nevertheless, when we see David in the Book of Acts, it isn't his failure that is remembered. In chapter 13 we are told, "I have found David, son of Jesse, a man after my own heart" (Acts 13:22 NIV). And then again in verse 36 it says David served "God's purposes in his own generation."

When David's life was rehearsed for the generations to remember, it was not the rogue brush stroke of adultery chronicled in the Book of Acts. Yes, he sinned and, yes, he stumbled. But his character was bigger than one slip and fall. For David, the overall pattern was a man who pursued the heart of God.

David had to carry some consequences of his sin the rest of his life. But there is a difference between someone slipping once and someone who repeats the behavior over and over creating a groove in their character.

We must realize that we ARE going to mess up. It is what we do with that mess-up that cuts the groove in our character. Abraham Lincoln once said, "My great concern is not whether you have failed, but whether you are content with your failure." It's not so much failure that forms character, but what we do after failure. Do we cover it up, ignore it, deny it, or do we admit it, walk toward it, and embrace personal change?

David is a good example of setting and raising the character standard. Despite serious sins, the way he dealt with his relationship to God and with other people and his own sin gives us a picture of a man after God's own heart.

✵ TAKING ACTION

1. Finish the following statement: Character is . . .

_____

_____

_____

2. Which would be a better character assessment tool: a Polaroid camera or a video camera with an eight-hour tape? Why do you say so?

_____

_____

_____

3. Why is character so important?

_____

_____

_____

4. If character is defined as: "*the sum of all I have done, both public and private, arranged as patterns across the entire spectrum of my life,*" how would you rate your character on a scale of 1 to 10 (ten being of the highest integrity)?

_____

_____

_____

5. Refresh your memory on the four lessons on character and then answer the questions that follow:

- **Lesson One: Take ownership of your character (Job 27:5, 6)**
  Character is one area of life in which we have a great amount of control. Do you daily choose to have sterling and firm character?

  _____

  _____

- **Lesson Two: Start your pattern early and don't let up (Gal. 6:7)**
  Question from the past: How have your early years established character flaws/strengths?

  _____

  _____

  Question from the present: Are you thinking, acting, and practicing things of integrity?

  _____

  _____

- **Lesson Three: Over-manage your Achilles (2 Cor. 12:9)**
  We all struggle with one or two sins of the heart that are unique to our makeup. What temptation or temptations make up your Achilles heel? How can you protect yourself from it?

  _____

  _____

- **Lesson Four: Character is not about perfection (1 John 1:8, 9)**
We must realize that we ARE going to mess up. It is what we do with that mess-up that cuts the groove in our character. Is there a failure you have not dealt with in your life?

_____

_____

CHAPTER 16

No Overnight Delivery on Character

"YOU CANNOT DREAM YOURSELF INTO A CHARACTER; YOU MUST HAMMER AND FORGE YOURSELF ONE."

—JAMES A. FROUDE

❋ DRIVING THOUGHT

Character is a fruit of the heart.

❋ DRILLING DOWN

Grigori Aleksandrovich Potemkin was an eighteenth-century Russian minister to the Czarina Catherine the Great. In 1789, Catherine decided to tour her empire down the Dneiper River through the Ukriane and Crimea. To impress Catherine with his administration of the region, Potemkin ordered a thorough sprucing up of everything along the way. The countryside was furiously whitewashed. In their zeal to make a favorable impression on Catherine, however, Potemkin's bureaucrats created whole new villages that consisted of pasteboard facades. They were a sham, a fraud.

Is your morality a "Potemkin village"?

Without the spiritual regeneration of God's spirit, our best attempts at goodness and morality are no better. They may fool others, but they lack the substance of real character. They are but feeble imitations. The framework for our heart to grow sound character comes only after God has touched it and turned it inside out.

When Jesus was preparing His team of leaders for the adversity that He knew would come, He explained character development this way, "No good tree bears bad fruit, nor does a bad tree bear good fruit. The good man brings good things out of the good stored up in his heart, and the evil man brings evil things out of the evil stored up in his heart" (Luke 6:43, 45 NIV). Character is a fruit of the heart.

The conventional wisdom of leadership sees character as a muscle of leadership. In truth, character is a muscle of the heart. Our culture is enamored with leadership when it should be enamored with character.

Every legitimate survey done in the last few years consistently shows that integrity, honesty, and credibility are common characteristics of superior leaders. Our culture, however, tries in vain to build a good heart apart from God. It's like trying to create a rainbow without resorting to beauty. The two are synonymous. One is the substance of the other.

We cannot acquire these qualities simply by reading a book on "virtue" or listening to another speech on "being a successful leader." Good leaders have character that has grown from the soil of a good heart.

Apart from God's spiritual intervention in our lives, the most we can muster in the heart is a Potemkin village of morality.

MAKING EVALUATION

If character is what counts most, then it is critical that we build and protect a strong, pure heart. As the Book of Proverbs says, "As the heart goes, so we go." The heart is where character is forged. After God gives us a new heart, it is up to us to water and nurture it. There are four factors to fostering a good heart that yields a bumper crop of good character. All four ingredients are necessary. Bypass any of them and character is short-circuited. Let's examine each of these components.

1. Right Thinking

Not long after GPS came into wide usage as a navigation tool for ships, an odd thing happened. Maritime insurance companies noticed an increase in the loss claims due to ships running aground. Navigation had never been easier, never been more precise. Why would a technological revolution that removed so many barriers to safety lead to such catastrophic failures?

The reason, it turned out was simple. Many captains, it seems, stopped looking at the map. They punched destination coordinates into the GPS and put the ship on autopilot. Not unlike the business world, they thought technology would give them an easy ride. But while GPS took their ship on a straight line from point A to point B just as it had been told, it couldn't read maps. No one was thinking. And with no one thinking, ships ran aground.

Working without faith is like using a GPS without reference to a map. We may be in motion. We might be getting somewhere. But we had better prepare for a jarring wake up when we hit the hard-wired moral reality of the cosmos.

Many people redefine right and wrong on the job to suit their present needs, then wonder why they run aground. They are working on a faulty definition of honesty or integrity or diligence or loyalty. The problem is their lack of right thinking.

Faith provides the critical moral map to our work. It tells us how to think rightly about what we are doing. How consistently do you consult your faith map during your daily Life@Work?

2. TIME

Time is either your friend or your enemy, depending on how you have spent it. Time is the enemy of a life wasted, but it is the friend of a life that's been consistently invested.

In the area where I live, land is constantly being cleared for new subdivisions. The trees are cut down, leaving bald earth. Then the houses are built. Finally, new landscaping is put in. Store-bought trees, however, are pathetic when compared to the mature specimens that had once grown there. It takes years for a full gloried maple or oak tree to sprawl across someone's front yard. And it takes years for mature character to be built. As Samuel Johnson said, "Excellence, in any department, can only be attained by the labor of a lifetime. It is not purchased at a lesser price."

Time builds character, and time tests character.

Are you making the daily investments in your character that will allow it to grow over time?

3. PRESSURE

It usually takes years for the natural course of a river to turn. Year after year erosion cuts its banks, creating new and different paths. If, however, you take the same river and apply the sustained pressure from a flood, its course could change in days. Fly over the Mississippi and you will see telltale remnants of such catastrophic change. It meanders like a snake, but all along its course are the oxbow lakes and channels of its former riverbed. When the rains come and the water rises, there is always a new landscape after it recedes back into its banks.

The pressures of life change our character—for good or bad.

The epistle of James says it this way: "Consider it pure joy, my brothers, whenever you face trials of many kinds, because you know that the testing of your faith develops perseverance. Perseverance must finish its work so that you may be mature and complete, not lacking anything" (James 1:2–4 NIV). Tough times come to all of us. Different shapes, different sizes, different weights, but they will come. The Bible acknowledges that as a fact of life on this planet. How we receive and digest suffering can become one of the greatest shapers of our character.

How has suffering shaped your character?

4. Good Decisions

Character development many times comes down to a single choice. It is the instant when we have to choose the good over the bad, the right over the wrong and the true over the false.

The ability to make right decisions is "wisdom." Wisdom is knowledge rightly applied. Character results from a series of wise decisions. Choosing wisely requires not only knowledge, but also discernment. It also requires the fortitude to do what ought to be done no matter how difficult it is. And real wisdom looks for what is right, what is best, what is good, no matter what the consequences or opposition. Finally, a good decision needs timely execution. There is always a tipping point at which the benefit of more analysis is outweighed by the opportunity cost of delay. Yes, committing ourselves to one option closes the door on others. Hesitation, however, is a habit of poor character.

Decision-making is a muscle. It atrophies when not used. It must become an instinct. A will to act and act wisely is at the core of what character means. Leo J. Muir concurred when he wrote, "Character is a subtle thing. Its sources are obscure, its roots delicate and invisible. We know it when we see it and it always commands our admiration, and the absence of it our pity; but it is largely a matter of will." There is no character where there is no will to act.

What kind of shape are your decision-making muscles in?

✸ TAKING ACTION

1. What role does your relationship with God play in your development of character?

   _____

   _____

2. What are some ways people try to develop character apart from God?

   _____

   _____

3. In what ways has your character resembled a "Potemkin village"?

   _____

   _____

4. Respond to the following questions about the four key ingredients in developing good character:

A. Right Thinking. Faith provides the critical moral map to our work. It tells us how to think rightly about what we are doing. How consistently do you consult your faith map during your daily Life@Work?

_____

_____

_____

B. Time. It takes years to build mature character. Time builds character and time tests character, as well. How are you making the daily investments in your character that will allow it to grow over time?

_____

_____

_____

C. Pressure. The pressures of life change our character—for good or bad. How we receive and digest suffering can become one of the greatest shapers of our character. How has suffering shaped your character?

_____

_____

_____

D. Good Decisions. Character development many times comes down to a single choice. It is the instant when we have to choose the good over the bad, the right over the wrong and the true over the false. Are you strong enough to make the right choices?

_____

_____

_____

**Right Thinking + Time + Pressure + Good Decisions =
Good Character**

5. Name a situation in which a strong character that has been nurtured over time can be absolutely necessary for survival:

_____

_____

_____

CHAPTER 17

Constructing a Moral Warehouse

"EFFECTIVENESS WITHOUT VALUES IS A TOOL WITHOUT A PURPOSE."

—EDWARD DE BONO

❂ DRIVING THOUGHT

A well-stocked moral warehouse provides the critical infrastructure for distributing a character-driven Life@Work.

❂ DRILLING DOWN

Sam Walton defied the odds. While other mass retailers were hemorrhaging financially, Walton built the Wal-Mart® empire—the world's largest chain of general merchandise stores.

Walton's stores were big, open, and clean, with a smiling face greeting customers at the door. His discount prices were not blue-light specials, an exception to the rule. Instead, everything in the store was sold as cheaply as he could sell it. Walton pulled off what no other retailer in the world ever did quite so well: offering everything customers needed, in stock and at their fingertips, and all at "Everyday Low Prices."

Wal-Mart took over like kudzu. From one store in Rogers, Arkansas in

1962, it now has more than forty-three hundred associated facilities around the globe. In 2003, Wal-Mart became the number one Fortune 500 Company. In 2004, it was rated one of the most admired companies in America. It must be doing something right.

There is a secret to Wal-Mart's success that isn't seen in its stores: the Wal-Mart warehouse. Two contradictory facts have long haunted retail. On the one hand, a store can't sell a product it doesn't stock. On the other hand, inventory costs money. Wal-Mart solved this dilemma by developing a state-of-the-art warehousing and distribution system using technology resulting in just-in-time delivery.

A Wal-Mart warehouse and distribution center is something to behold. Eight-hundred-thousand square feet of warehousing space sit on fifty acres of land. Truckloads of goods constantly come in and out at forty-five plus shipping docks. Six-hundred employees work day and night, receiving, tracking, and dispatching freight. On any given day, the warehouse handles $10 million in inventory. In a year, Wal-Mart's warehouses ship more than $240 billion of merchandise worldwide.

Wal-Mart invests $55 million to construct each of its distribution centers for one reason: You have to stock before you can sell.

This simple principle is just as true for our work lives. Character has to have a moral warehouse. Constructing a moral warehouse is a critical infrastructure for God-intended Life@Work. If we have no systems in place that keep our souls well-stocked, we shouldn't be surprised when we find the shelves empty.

A moral warehouse is not just static virtue. Just like warehousing and distribution, character depends on an ongoing process. It constantly needs replenishing. Its inventory needs ongoing management.

Too often, those who discuss moral character only talk about the virtues themselves—honesty, loyalty, perseverance, courage, etc.—while neglecting the process by which such personal strengths are acquired and built into one's life. Similarly, building a successful Life@Work is more about having a moral warehouse filled with solid life habits than it is about the specific character qualities themselves.

MAKING EVALUATION

Wal-Mart's warehousing and distribution system includes huge warehouses, fleets of trucks, cutting-edge tracking software, and solid management. Four activities are equally critical in the construction, filling, and management of our moral warehouses: Constructing personal convictions, capturing inspirational moments, conducting Scripture memory, and connecting with people of character.

Take some time and check your warehousing and distribution system.

CONSTRUCTING PERSONAL CONVICTIONS

It has been said that an opinion is something you hold whereas a conviction is something that holds you. But what is a conviction? Here's our definition: *A conviction is a category of God's thinking on a particular area or issue that I wholeheartedly embrace and act upon with determination.*

Our warehouses need to be stocked with timeless axioms and values that don't change. The only place to get an unbiased perspective not subject to human whim is from God. Thankfully, we don't need to sit around and wonder about God's thinking because it's recorded in the Bible.

Have you developed any convictions that shape and guide your work life? What are they? Write out the ten most active convictions that apply to your work life. Make sure they are rooted in the Scripture. Without them, you will be what James describes as "a doubtful mind is as unsettled as a wave of the sea that is driven and tossed by the wind" (James 1:6 NLT).

CAPTURING INSPIRATIONAL MOMENTS OF LIFE

There are times and moments in life that are pregnant with meaning: the birth of a child, graduations, weddings, funerals, promotions, layoffs, achievements, or perhaps failures. These are times when something externally causes us to pull over for some internal reflection. We pause and drink in life a little slower than usual.

These transformational encounters provide the chance to inventory our moral warehouse. It could be sitting out on the porch watching the sun go down. It could be a close call or an accident. It could be a scare or a thrill. It could be attached to a day away or a vacation. A song can do it. A sight can trigger it. A memory can hit the switch. An annual review could do it.

Transformational moments are born from both tragedies and personal triumphs. The point is not the drama but the teachable moment that life provides.

We pause, inhale, and contemplate. It is a time when we reorder our private world, a time when we realign our belief system with our behavior. It is at these moments in life that we do some of our best character review and character alignment.

CONDUCTING SCRIPTURE MEMORY

It's no overstatement to suggest that we now have a whole cohort growing up without a firsthand knowledge of the Scripture. Modern worship and progressive churches provide much-needed practical sermons and fun, creative narratives, but too often we no longer engage the Scriptures directly.

Scripture memory is not difficult. Like working out, it just requires an investment of a few minutes each day. There are many resources designed to get you started. But you can easily begin on your own. Stop and make a list of the current concerns on your plate of life: perhaps a difficult boss, your son's bad grades, conflict with your husband over finances, a test report of cancer present, the uncertainty of a job transition. Now take these concerns to Scripture.

Unfortunately, many people still see the Bible as a book for preachers to stand on for a Sunday sermon or a collection of Christian super heroes only for children. It's much, much more. It also provides wisdom, guidance, and encouragement for each of us every day in the details of life.

CONNECTING WITH PEOPLE OF CHARACTER

Good character keeps good company.

We all know this to be true when we are young; we just forget that it's still true as we get older. Remember the kids in your neighborhood that your mom told you to stay away from? "He's a rotten apple," she would say. (Of course, we wonder how many moms were saying that about us back then.) We all know what that means. It means the same thing that Paul meant when he said decisively, "Bad company corrupts good character" (1 Cor. 15:33 NIV). But who cautions us of rotten apples when life graduates us to our twenties, thirties, forties, and beyond?

Sit down and analyze all the relationships in your personal world. In honor of your mother, sort them into four apple categories: Healthy apples, bruised apples, rotten apples, and poisonous apples.

In which bucket of apples are you spending the most time? Remember, healthy relationships reinforce strong character and unhealthy relationships destroy it.

❋ TAKING ACTION

1. How can we compare our morality to a warehouse?

   _____

   _____

   _____

2. Are you regularly investing in your moral warehouse? What are some specific ways you can invest in your warehouse?

   _____

   _____

   _____

3. What is a conviction?

   _____

   _____

4. Name five of your top ten convictions and if possible write a corresponding scriptural reference beside it:

a. _____

b. _____

c. _____

d. _____

e. _____

5. Name a place or situation in which your convictions are challenged or tested.

_____

_____

_____

6. Name a few ways that your convictions are counter-cultural.

_____

_____

_____

7. How can you display your convictions without being obnoxious?

_____

_____

_____

_____

8. What consequences might your convictions bring?

_____

_____

_____

9. Have you had an "inspirational moment" that caused you to inventory what is important to you in life? What was the moment? What did you learn?

_____

_____

_____

10. According to 1 Corinthians 15:33, "Bad company corrupts good character." Another way to put it, "One rotten apple can spoil the whole bunch." Which of the following phrases best describes your community?

healthy apples   rotten apples

bruised apples   poisonous apples

CHAPTER 18

THE CHURCH@WORK

"I BELIEVE ONE OF THE NEXT GREAT MOVES OF GOD IS GOING TO BE THROUGH THE BELIEVERS IN THE WORKPLACE."

—DR. BILLY GRAHAM

⊛ DRIVING THOUGHT

The next decade will be memorialized by the churches that celebrate and equip people to live an impacting and effective Life@Work.

⊛ DRILLING DOWN

Eighteen months after my first encounter with him in a Chicago boardroom, a report came my way on our old friend, Charles Antonio Bordini III. I am happy to report he was still going full throttle. He was still very much commercial, still very much kingdom—still very much Charlie. Only now he was living and working a life that was whole. The good news is that Charlie is one of a growing legion of Christians across the country who is rediscovering the doubly sharp Life@Work for which God made him.

As it's been for Charlie, it is critical that we correctly see and sort the four landscapes of church life, family life, civic life, and work life. Why? If we think that our commercial worlds are only there to support, resource, and platform the professional ministry of the church, we will undercut our callings and have no incentive to keep our skill sets sharp. If we see our jobs as the enemy of our churches or families, we will always operate in a vocation shortfall. If all we see of our work is a paycheck, we will not view it as part of our wider involvement with our communities. If we don't squarely stake down what work can and should do for us, it will run recklessly across the other parts of our Life@Work. It is impossible to sustain a balanced and successful Life@Work without putting church, family, community, and work in their proper arrangement.

As Charlie learned, work itself must be reforged, integrating our kingdom commitments with our commercial callings. To do that we must understand, appreciate, and approach work correctly. It was the world of work where Charlie was facing his painful disconnect. It was there that Charlie had to navigate the myths and misconceptions that often derail even the most purposeful followers of Jesus.

Through understanding and employing the four quiet but powerful tools of Delivering Skill, Evidencing Calling, Modeling Serving, and Displaying Character, we can flesh out the ideas of integration and impact. Those four tools open the box of optimum internal fulfillment, external maximum impact, and passionate pleasure in God.

MAKING EVALUATION

So, what does it look like when we're using all four tools? What's the picture of our Life@Work when we deliver skill, evidence calling, model serving, and display character? What do others see when we're achieving proficiency in our careers but also in our walks with Christ—when we know Scripture as well as we know balance sheets?

Some might say it looks like a balanced Life@Work, but it's really something much, much more. This isn't the type of balance where each competing element gets equal weight. It's an integration of all those things, so that they fit together and work together in a way that gives life a more complete mission and meaning.

We call this objective a "very, very" life, and it's something we can strive for as individuals and in community.

ARE YOU LIVING A VERY, VERY LIFE?

If you critique your daily lifestyle for "very, very" living—a life that's very Bible and very business—what will you find? Many folks we meet are "very business, sort of Bible" or "sort of business, very Bible." A "very, very" person consistently develops a growing expertise in both Bible and business. Being successful in Life@Work is all about exploring and understanding a "very, very" world and becoming a "very, very" disciple with both confidence and credibility.

New believers are the only people with a legitimate reason to say, "I don't know the Bible very well." Anyone who has been in the faith for a few years ought to know the Book, regardless of whether he receives a paycheck from a church or has attended seminary. The accountant should know Numbers as well as she knows numbers. The attorney should know Judges as well as he knows judges. And the politician should know First and Second Kings as well as he knows his favorite legislative kingpins.

Jesus was not "sort of human, very godlike" or "very human and kind of godlike." Jesus' spirituality and His humanity were seamless. He wasn't a "great rabbi" but just an "okay carpenter." Mark describes Jesus as a *tekton*, a "technician," a master of His craft. Jesus knew how to turn out an excellent product, and He knew how to turn a profit. For Him, it was all a part of working as a servant of God in the marketplace. He was "very, very," and so, too, should we be.

ARE YOU LIVING IN A VERY, VERY COMMUNITY?

Bob Briner, our late friend and the longtime president of ProServ Television, came from humble beginnings and made his way through the ranks of the highly competitive world of professional sports. He was a "player" and he was in the game, but he found himself woefully unprepared to integrate his faith in Jesus with his work.

"As I searched for help in combining Christian living with my world of professional sports and television, it didn't come from my church or denomination," Briner wrote in *Roaring Lambs,* a groundbreaking book challenging believers to impact culture through their work (*Roaring Lambs,* p. 15).

While schools and professional associates trained him well to excel in his work, he didn't find much training on how to be a follower of Jesus in it—unless he wanted to become a pastor or a missionary.

For too long the church has operated as a nursing home and not as a boot camp. In a nursing home, people move in but they never move out. In a boot camp, we are trained to move out every day, to hit the deck running.

The reason people never move out of the church is that the Christian subculture has given up on our culture. We no longer value or prioritize Christian contributions to human endeavor. The church, as Briner noted, "is almost a nonentity when it comes to shaping culture. In the arts, entertainment, media, education, and other culture-shaping venues of our country, the church has abdicated its role as salt and light" (*Roaring Lambs,* p. 28).

The winds of change, however, are shifting. It is no longer about Unchurched Harry and Mary; it is about Unconnected Unfulfilled Charlie. Reaching and Empowering Charlie is the transformer for the church of tomorrow. A movement of God is afoot in the workplace. Henry Blackaby has declared, "I've never seen the activity of God this deeply in the business community as I do right now." A worldwide spiritual movement is growing in the workplace. It didn't start in the church, but rather in what the New Testament called the Agora, the marketplace. It was in the marketplace where life traveled in the first century, and it is in the Agora where life intersects today.

The church, remember, is the body of Christ. It's not a building. And we are part of that body. So the question is, where are we taking the body of Christ? Is it living in the workplace, impacting the community? Are we helping to create momentum in this movement?

✺ TAKING ACTION

1. What are the dangers of an unbalanced view of the areas of work, family, and church? What could result in the over/under valuing of any given one?

_____

_____

2. What is a "very, very" person? Are you there? Where do you need to grow?

_____

_____

_____

3. If the church is the dugout and the workplace is the field upon which we play the game, describe what the end results of each place should look like.

_____

_____

_____

4. What role should the church play in making an impact in the workplace?

_____

_____

_____

5. In what ways has the church missed the opportunity of maximizing the effectiveness of Christians in the workplace?

_____

_____

_____

6. Name three ways your church could help you in your Life@Work:

    a. _____

    b. _____

    c. _____

7. Name three ways you can use your Life@Work to build the kingdom of God:

   a. _____

   b. _____

   c. _____

8. What potential impact could you envision from an inspired and trained group of businessmen and women who implement their faith@work?

   _____

   _____

   _____

   _____

9. In light of our discussion on the four emphasized tools of integrating our faith@work, name one lasting insight you gained from each one during your study:

   Delivering Skill

   _____

   _____

   _____

   Evidencing Calling

   _____

   _____

   _____

Modeling Serving

_____

_____

Displaying Character

_____

_____

Notes

CHAPTER 15

1. Oswald Sanders, *Bible Men of Faith* (Chicago: Moody, 1965), 121.

CHAPTER 18

1. Bob Briner, *Roaring Lambs* (Grand Rapids: Zondervan, 1993), 15.

Some information not specifically endnoted was found on the following websites:

www.creativequotations.com
www.famous quotes.com
www.quotationpage.com

ABOUT THE AUTHORS

JOHN C. MAXWELL, known as America's expert on leadership, speaks in person to hundreds of thousands of people each year. He has communicated his principles to Fortune 500 companies, the United States Military Academy at West Point, international marketing organizations, the NCAA, and professional sports groups such as the NFL. Maxwell is the founder of several leadership organizations, including Maximum Impact, helping people reach their personal and leadership potential. A *New York Times* best-selling author, Dr. Maxwell has written more than thirty books, including *Developing the Leader Within You, Thinking for a Change, There's No Such Thing as Business Ethics,* and *The 21 Irrefutable Laws of Leadership,* which has sold more than one million copies.

STEPHEN R. GRAVES and THOMAS G. ADDINGTON have been business partners and best friends for almost two decades. For the last fifteen years, they have been exploring how to blend business excellence with biblical wisdom through consulting, teaching, mentoring, and writing. This mission statement, originally scratched out on a breakfast napkin early one morning fourteen years ago, has been their "never lost" system as they have journeyed through a variety of entrepreneurial endeavors and experiments.

They founded Cornerstone Consulting Group, The WellSpring Group and the *Life@Work Journal;* they speak regularly in business, ministry, and academic settings; they publish frequently; serve on national boards; and they are active in coaching leaders toward the finish line. Both hold earned doctorates, both are deeply devoted to their families, and both love the never-ending challenge of meshing real life with the message of Jesus. They have authored fifteen books or booklets.

BOOKS BY DR. JOHN C. MAXWELL
CAN TEACH YOU HOW TO BE A REAL SUCCESS

RELATIONSHIPS
Be a People Person (Victor Books)
Becoming a Person of Influence (Nelson Business)
The Power of Influence (Honor Books)
The Power of Partnership in the Church (J. Countryman)
Relationships 101 (Nelson Business)
The Treasure of a Friend (J. Countryman)
Winning with People (Nelson Business)

EQUIPPING
Developing the Leaders Around You (Nelson Business)
Equipping 101 (Nelson Business)
Partners in Prayer (Nelson Business)
Your Road Map for Success (Nelson Business)
Your Road Map for Success Workbook (Nelson Business)
Success One Day at a Time (J. Countryman)
The 17 Indisputable Laws of Teamwork (Nelson Business)
The 17 Essential Qualities of a Team Player (Nelson Business)

ATTITUDE
Be All You Can Be (Victor Books)
Failing Forward (Nelson Business)
The Power of Thinking (Honor Books)
Living at the Next Level (Nelson Business)
Think on These Things (Beacon Hill)
The Winning Attitude (Nelson Business)
Your Bridge to a Better Future (Nelson Business)
The Power of Attitude (Honor Books)

LEADERSHIP
The 21 Indispensable Qualities of a Leader (Nelson Business)
The 21 Irrefutable Laws of Leadership (Nelson Business)
The 21 Most Powerful Minutes in a Leader's Day (Nelson Business)
Developing the Leader Within You Workbook (Nelson Business)
Developing the Leader Within You (Nelson Business)
The Power of Leadership (Honor Books)
The Right to Lead (J. Countryman)

OTHER TITLES BY
STEPHEN GRAVES AND THOMAS ADDINGTON

Life@Work: Marketplace Success for People of Faith

The Power of One

Clout: Tapping Spiritual Wisdom to Become a Person of Influence

Deep Focus: Devotions for Living the Word

Behind the Bottom Line: Powering Business Life with Spiritual Wisdom

Life@Work on Leadership: Enduring Insights for Men and Women of Faith

Daily Focus: Daily Readings for Integrating Faith in the Workplace

The Building Block Series

Framing Your Ambition
The Hard Work of Rest
Cornerstones for Calling
Ethical Anchors
The Mentoring Blueprint

The Fourth Frontier: Exploring the New World of Work

Notes

_____
_____
_____
_____
_____
_____
_____
_____
_____
_____
_____
_____
_____
_____
_____

NOTES

NOTES

_____

_____

_____

_____

_____

_____

_____

_____

_____

_____

_____

_____

_____

_____

Notes

NOTES

_____

_____

_____

_____

_____

_____

_____

_____

_____

_____

_____

_____

_____

NOTES

_____

_____

_____

_____

_____

_____

_____

_____

_____

_____

_____

_____

_____

_____

_____

_____

NOTES

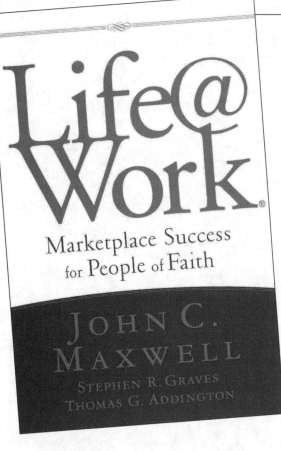

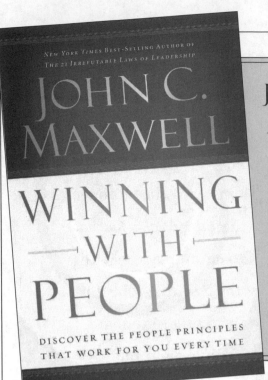

JOHN C. MAXWELL, AMERICA'S LEADERSHIP EXPERT, PROVIDES THE TWENTY-FIVE ESSENTIAL PEOPLE PRINCIPLES THAT LEAD TO SUCCESSFUL BUSINESS AND PERSONAL RELATIONSHIPS.

Ask successful CEOs, entrepreneurs, salespeople, and pastors what characteristic is most needed for success in leadership positions, and they'll tell you—it's the ability to work with people.

Maxwell has divided the People Principles in this book according to the questions you must ask yourself if you want to win with people:

→ Readiness: Are you prepared for relationships?
→ Connection: Are you willing to focus on others?
→ Trust: Can you build mutual trust?
→ Investment: Are you willing to invest in others?
→ Synergy: Can you create win-win relationships?

Some people are born with great relationship skills, but those who are not can learn to improve them. In *Winning with People* Maxwell has translated decades of experience into 25 People Principles that anyone can learn.

NELSON BUSINESS
A Division of Thomas Nelson Publishers
Since 1798
www.thomasnelson.com

NOW AVAILABLE
WHEREVER BOOKS ARE SOLD!

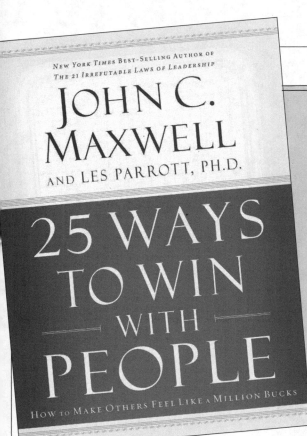

Introducing the Complete Life@Work Ministry Program!

Let the *Life@Work* Program help you generate enormous buzz and goodwill in your community! By hosting a simulcast once a year for the business professionals in your area, your church will have the foundation in place to provide a **powerful outreach program** aimed at merging faith into the workplace to impact your neighborhood.

Launching a ministry of this caliber for this audience has been a daunting task in the past — mainly because very few resources exist that have real meaning to busy business professionals. Current work resources that are available rarely hit home for participants and poorly relate to real business issues. Solving this problem has been the mission for *Life@Work* and we believe the *Life@Work* **Program is the definitive answer.**

Your church ministry or small group can pick and choose what portions of the program best fit their mission as well. The *Life@Work* Program includes: **The *Life@Work* Groupzine series, *Life@Work* resources, *Life@Work* Simulcast, *Life@Work* Symposium,** and additional modules and training will be available over time. Select the programs that best fit your needs and finances and begin building your workplace ministry outreach today!

Life@Work
Resources

To make a continued, reverberating impact in the marketplace, we need faith-friendly resources that add immense value to a business professional. *Life@Work* resources include various training programs by best-selling author John C. Maxwell. *Learning the 21 Irrefutable Laws of Leadership, Winning With People,* and *Learning the 17 Indisputable Laws of Teamwork* DVD training courses are excellent programs your workplace ministry can host that can attract additional businesspeople.

This training also adds value to your church's current crop of business leaders — allowing them to see that your church has their needs and personal growth in mind.

   Additional resources are planned and being developed that will help provide continual training for a workplace ministry leader and those who take part in the training.

   Please visit **www.lifeatwork.com** for additional information and updates on upcoming resource and training releases.

Life@Work
Simulcast

There is no better way to make an instant, powerful impact among the business professionals in your community than with a proven leadership training event featuring some of the greatest business minds and leaders of our time. Previous speakers at this event have included: **John Wooden, Pat Summitt, Lou**  **Holtz, Joe Gibbs, Ken Blanchard, Brian Tracy, Zig Ziglar, and John C. Maxwell.** Broadcast in over 500 churches each year, this LIVE training event is the ideal catalyst to launch your workplace ministry.

Dispel the notion that your church is out of touch with 21st century professionals and draw in the business leaders in your community. This event will define your church as **the church** in your area **known for taking care of business.**

Life@Work
Symposium

The most crucial aspect of any ministry is the struggle to maintain a relevant edge amongst its participants. Picture a current singles group using material and teaching styles from 1970 (scary, isn't it?). Remaining current allows a ministry to continually grow. Even more so, a workplace ministry must remain relevant. Business professionals

won't sacrifice the time unless the material "delivers the goods." To remain on the forefront, *Life@Work* created the *Life@Work* **Symposium.** This gathering includes pastors, key workplace ministry leaders, business professionals, and noted experts to provide training for workplace ministry leaders and generate up-to-date, relevant content and study materials for the business professional.

Symposium participants will walk away from this event equipped and encouraged with resources and follow-up strategies for reaching their laity as well as the business community. Workplace ministry leaders are given a strategic plan to teach to and connect with the members of the study. Consider this Symposium experience a crash course in "*Wall Street Journal* meets Scripture."

Learn more about the *Life@Work* **Symposium** at www.lifeatwork.com.